Text and illustrations copyright The Estate of Mrs J. C. Heath Robinson 1982.

First published in Great Britain 1912 by Constable & Co.
First published in Great Britain 1924 by Hodder & Stoughton.
This edition published 1982 reproduced from the original edition.

ISBN 0 340 27732 7 (standard)
ISBN 0 340 27965 6 (leather)

All rights reserved. No part of this publication may be
reproduced or transmitted in any form or by any means,
electronic or mechanical, including photocopy, recording, or
any information storage and retrieval system, without
permission in writing from the publisher.

Published by Hodder & Stoughton Children's Books,
(a division of Hodder & Stoughton Ltd.)
Mill Road, Dunton Green, Sevenoaks, Kent TN13 2YJ.

Printed in Great Britain by T. J. Press (Padstow) Ltd.
Colour plates by Sackville Press Billericay Ltd.
Bound by Dorstel Press Ltd., Harlow, Essex.

CONTENTS

CONTENTS

	PAGE
BILL THE MINDER	1
THE KING OF TROY	15
THE ANCIENT MARINER	33
THE TRIPLETS	51
GOOD AUNT GALLADIA	65
THE DOCTOR	79
THE RESPECTABLE GENTLEMAN	97
THE SICILIAN CHAR-WOMAN	115
THE INTERVAL	133
THE REAL SOLDIER	147
THE WILD MAN	165
THE MUSICIAN	183

CONTENTS

	PAGE
THE LOST GROCER	199
THE MERCHANT'S WIFE	213
THE CAMP-FOLLOWERS	227
THE SIEGE OF TROY	241
THE END	255

LIST OF ILLUSTRATIONS

COLOURED PLATES

FRONTISPIECE		
THE KING OF TROY COMPELLED TO ASK HIS WAY	*To face page*	30
THE SPORT OF EVERY MER-KID	,,	48
HE WAS ALWAYS AT HAND	,,	58
I FELL FROM MY POSITION	,,	72
THE LORD MAYOR HELD A LONG COUNCIL	,,	88
THE RESPECTABLE GENTLEMAN	,,	110
BASIL HERBERT DEVELOPS A CHILBLAIN	,,	122
AND LEFT HIM TO HAVE HIS CRY OUT	,,	140
REGINALD COMPLETELY LOST HIS TEMPER	,,	156
HARMLESS INDEED WERE OUR JOYS	,,	168
AND PLAYED IT FOR MY DELIGHT	,,	190
FOLLOWED HIM AT THE GREATEST SPEED	,,	208
BRINGING WITH THEM A LITTLE OLD MAN	,,	216
THEY CAME UPON A GREAT STONE SPHINX	,,	230
CLOSELY OBSERVED FROM THE WATCH TOWERS	,,	244

BILL THE MINDER

	PAGE
TITLE-PAGE	1
HEADPIECE	2
HIS HOWLS BECAME TERRIFIC	7
ALWAYS INVENTING NEW WAYS OF MINDING	10
YOUNG TOOTH-CUTTERS FORGOT THEIR TROUBLES	11
THE ONLY MINDER OF THE DISTRICT	13
TAILPIECE	14

LIST OF ILLUSTRATIONS

THE KING OF TROY

	PAGE
TITLE-PAGE	15
HEADPIECE	16
HE CLIMBED THE RICK	18
HE COMMENCED HIS TALE	21
WHAT A TIME WE HAD	26
TAILPIECE	31
VIGNETTE	32

THE ANCIENT MARINER

TITLE-PAGE	33
HEADPIECE	34
I SIGN ON AS CABIN BOY	39
I WENT ON WITH MY SANDWICHES	42
FOR YEARS WE SAILED	47
TAILPIECE	49
VIGNETTE	50

THE TRIPLETS

TITLE-PAGE	51
HEADPIECE	52
ENDEAVOURING TO COMFORT THE OLD MAN	55
WE GREW UP IN COMPARATIVE HAPPINESS	58
THE TRIPLETS ACCOMPANY THE ARMY	63
TAILPIECE	64

GOOD AUNT GALLADIA

TITLE-PAGE	65
HEADPIECE	66
I JUST MANAGED TO REACH THE EGGS	71
I ANGLE THE AIR	72
I ERECTED MY POLE ON THE SANDS	73
ITS OLD STATELY SELF AGAIN	75

LIST OF ILLUSTRATIONS

THE DOCTOR

	PAGE
TITLE-PAGE	79
HEADPIECE	80
FAR SOONER HAVE THE MUMPS	83
THE PUFF BAKER	87
TREATED WITH DELICIOUS JALAPS	88
AS SOME PATIENT PREPARED HIS DOSE	89
THE VERY SPARROWS GREW THIN	91
POSTCARD	94
POSTCARD	95
TAILPIECE	96

THE RESPECTABLE GENTLEMAN

TITLE-PAGE	97
HEADPIECE	
BOWING POLITELY TO THE PILLAR-BOXES	103
THE CHURCH STEEPLE HAD BEEN REMOVED	104
STANDING ALONE UPON THE WALLS	106
DANGLING BY HIS LEGS	109
TAILPIECE	113
VIGNETTE	114

THE SICILIAN CHAR-WOMAN

TITLE-PAGE	115
HEADPIECE	116
I TOOK LEAVE OF MY SORROWING FATHER	120
HARDLY DISGUISING HIS EFFORTS TO IGNORE ME	121
THEY WERE COMPELLED TO SEND FOR A PHYSICIAN	125
THE IMPROVEMENT WAS MAINTAINED	129
DISCOVERED A CLOVE KERNEL	130
VIGNETTE	132

LIST OF ILLUSTRATIONS

THE INTERVAL

	PAGE
TITLE-PAGE	133
HEADPIECE	134
I FELL ON TO THE PARSNIP	137
THEY ALL ONCE MORE STARTED ON THEIR ADVENTUROUS JOURNEY	138, 139
THE WHOLE CAMP WAS FAST ASLEEP	142
TAILPIECE	145
VIGNETTE	146

THE REAL SOLDIER

TITLE-PAGE	147
HEADPIECE	148
THE REAL SOLDIER	153
'BUT HOLD!' CRIED THE PRESIDENT	156
'YOUR FATE BE UPON YOUR OWN HEAD'	157
FLOUNDERING ABOUT IN THE SEA	159
IN EXPECTATION OF THEIR LEADER	161
TAILPIECE	163
VIGNETTE	164

THE WILD MAN

TITLE-PAGE	165
HEADPIECE	166
I PLEADED MY CASE	169
AND KILLED IT ON THE SPOT	173
WE COOKED ONE GREAT STEAK	177
TAILPIECE	181
VIGNETTE	182

THE MUSICIAN

TITLE-PAGE	183
HEADPIECE	184

LIST OF ILLUSTRATIONS

	PAGE
SHE NOW MADE OFF TO THE WOODS	189
HE WOULD CLIMB TO THE TOPMOST BRANCHES	190
SWEEPING THE DEAD LEAVES	195
WITH NO OTHER WEALTH THAN MY CONCERTINA	197
TAILPIECE	198

THE LOST GROCER

TITLE-PAGE	199
HEADPIECE	200
AFFECTED BY HIS STORY	205
PLUMP INTO THE RIVER WE WENT	206
THERE GREW IN FRONT OF ME A GREAT MOUND	209
SNEEZING AND SNEEZING	211

THE MERCHANT'S WIFE

TITLE-PAGE	213
HEADPIECE	214
MOPING ABOUT THE COMMON	219
KEPT HIM OUT OF MISCHIEF	223
GLORIOUS TARTS AND SWEETS	224
IT DIDN'T MATTER HOW MUCH YOU ATE	225
TAILPIECE	226

THE CAMP-FOLLOWERS

TITLE-PAGE	227
HEADPIECE	228
THE HEADS SERVED FOR DOLLS	233
YOU ARE NOW OUR ONLY HOPE	234
I FISHED AND FISHED AND FISHED	237
TAILPIECE	239
VIGNETTE	240

LIST OF ILLUSTRATIONS

THE SIEGE OF TROY

	PAGE
TITLE-PAGE	241
HEADPIECE	242
PLAN OF SIEGE	245
THESE PARCELS WERE NOW LABELLED	248
AND PACKED HIM OFF TO PERSIA	251
TROY BECAME THE HAPPIEST TOWN	253

THE END

VIGNETTE	256

BILL THE MINDER

BILL THE MINDER

OLD CRISPIN, the mushroom gatherer, and his good wife Chloe had ten children, and nine of them were bad-tempered. There was Chad, the youngest and most bad-tempered of the lot, Hannibal and Quentin the twins, Randall with the red head, Noah, Ratchett the short-sighted, Nero the worrit, weeping Biddulph and Knut. The only good-tempered child was a little girl named Boadicea.

It is well known that a boy usually takes after his father, and a girl after her mother, and these children were no exception to the rule, for the boys all resembled old Crispin, whose temper had been rather tried, poor man, by the early hours at which he had to rise, in order to gather the mushrooms when they were quite new and young. On the other hand, Boadicea could only have inherited her good-temper from Chloe, who without doubt was the most good-tempered dame alive.

Now it is quite true that any one who cares to rise early enough in the morning may gather mushrooms, and plenty of them, too, but those who do so only now and again, and merely for amusement, little know the hard life of the professional gatherer, or the skill and judgment he has to cultivate in order to carry on his work with any success.

In the course of time Crispin became so well skilled that he could not only tell a mushroom from a toadstool at the distance of two hundred yards, but his hearing became so acute that he could even hear them growing, and learnt to distinguish the sound of each as it broke through the earth. Indeed, he had no need for any alarm to wake him from his heavy slumbers and call him to his work in the fields. However cautiously a mushroom made its appearance, at its first rumble, old Crispin would jump from his hard bed, hastily dress himself, and, often without tasting a morsel of breakfast, be out of the house and on to the field in time to see the newcomer pop its head through the earth. This he would pick, and then he would hop about with his head on one side listening for others like some old starling listening for worms, at the same time mewing like a cat to frighten away the birds that prey on the mushrooms. He was then able to fill his basket with the very freshest crop and take them round to people's houses in time for breakfast.

With such anxious work it will be readily understood that few mushroom gatherers can remain in the best of health for many years, and it so happened that in time the anxieties connected with the gathering of mushrooms began to affect old Crispin, so that he fell ill and completely lost his appetite. Chloe called in the doctor, but the latter at first could do nothing for him. He painted Crispin's chest and then his back with iodine; he rubbed him well with the roots of sarsaparilla; he made him sleep first on his right side, then on his left, and finally covered him in brown paper plasters and dock-leaf poultices and sent him to the sea-side with strict injunctions to take to sea-bathing, running, and aeroplaning, but it was all of no avail.

With the assistance of Boadicea, Chloe now tried to tempt her husband with every known and unknown dish, and when these failed, like a good wife, she invented others. She made trifles of vegetable marrow, tartlets of hen feathers to soothe the nerves, salads of spinach and carraway comfits, delicacies composed of porridge and mint, and the most luscious stews of pine-cones and lard. She then tried him with even lighter dishes, but it was no good. He became thinner and thinner every day, and his temper was growing shorter and shorter, when at last, to her great joy, she succeeded in making a jelly that really seemed to take his fancy.

At first there was little or no sign of improvement, yet he ate a very small portion of the jelly every day, and with this the anxious wife and daughter had to be contented for some time. He had remained in this state for weeks when Chloe resolved slightly to increase his portion. Finding that this did not disagree with him, but that, instead, he became a little stouter and a little better every day, she continued gradually giving him more and more.

At last she discovered that the more Crispin ate of this jelly, the greater his appetite became. In fact, if the truth be told, the old gentleman became in time not only quite well and very stout but also somewhat greedy. At all events, Chloe found that instead of being able to devote more time to her children, after restoring her husband's appetite, she had to give up more and more time to cooking. Crispin now spent the whole day in eating, and things went from bad to very bad, and from very bad to worse. Boadicea assisted her mother to the utmost, yet Chloe, worked almost to death, was at length compelled to look out for a minder, in order that her children might not be entirely neglected.

Many minders from all parts applied for employment, and, as a test of their skill, she set them the task of cheering the unfortunate Chad, who was cutting all his double teeth at the same time. Some tried to cheer him by singing to him, some by dancing to him; one even hoped to gladden the boy by jumping over him backwards and with a pleasant smile dropping on the grass in front of him. Again, some thought to distract him by running swiftly with him several times round the well, which only made him very ill. Another energetic young minder stood on his head in front of the child for at least ten minutes, which, instead of cheering the lad, nearly frightened him to death. One minder, more experienced than the rest, tried to make him forget his ache by giving him other aches to think of with the aid of a slipper, which he maintained he had succeeded in doing. However, he was not elected, for, try as they would, no one could discover for which ache the child was crying.

Many methods were tried, but none with even the smallest success; in fact, the competition greatly increased the child's discomfort. His howls became terrific, and so heartrending that, as a last resource, Chloe sent for her nephew Bill, who cleaned the boots. Now no one had suspected Bill of having the makings of a good minder in him, but it happened that he knew Chad's little ways, and so, to everybody's surprise and relief, he easily succeeded in keeping him quiet until all the double teeth had been cut. Thereupon he was at once elected Minder to the family.

BILL THE MINDER

HIS HOWLS BECAME TERRIFIC

Bill soon proved that he was no ordinary minder. Having once started on his new work, he took his profession very seriously. He read all the books that had ever been written upon the subject, which were to be found in the library of the British Museum. He talked about it with the most knowing professors of the subject, and he was as well known in the Minding Room of the Patent Museum at South Kensington as in his father's house. And it is even said that he once contrived to be shut in all night by hiding behind a case of red coral rattles when the policeman came round at dusk to shut and lock the doors.

Moreover, as you can see for yourselves in the

pictures, he was always inventing new ways of minding his charges. So expert did he become in time that he was never at a loss with the most fractious, and easily surpassing all rivals, he became the most perfect minder of the district.

Bill's fame spread to the most distant towns, and worried mothers for miles around flocked to him with their children. He was most successful in distracting the vaccinated, and under his care young tooth-cutters soon forgot their troubles. Even the pangs of indigestion were allayed and the fretfulness of the sleepless lulled to rest by the charm of his ways. Short tempers were lengthened, and terrified midnight wakers were taught to realise how ridiculous were their fears. Screechers ceased to screech, and grizzlers to grizzle, while weepers and howlers reformed their habits and learnt to chuckle throughout the day.

If any one could mind, Bill could!

But life was not all condensed milk and honey to Bill. Like all good minders and men, he had the bad fortune to arouse the jealousy of rivals. The unvarying success which met his clever treatment of the most difficult cases, instead of arousing the admiration of his brother minders, as one would have expected, and making them eager to imitate him, only had the effect of making them very cross and jealous. Some, indeed, became so wild that they had to be minded themselves, while others neglected their charges and wandered about the country in a dreadful state of grumpiness, biting their nails to the quick, and tearing their hair or anything else they could get hold of.

The time now arrived for the great annual Minding Tournament, held by the Duke to celebrate his birthday, to which every one had been looking forward all through the year. Few people have ever been so delighted over being born as was the Duke, and this was how he most liked to show his joy and thankfulness. The prizes and cups were usually subscribed for by the mothers and fathers, but this year was a very special occasion, for the Duke, having arrived at the age of sixty, had decided to present a gold-mounted feeding-bottle to be competed for during the tournament.

Everybody was there; the Duke and his Duchess with a handsome bouquet of marigolds and groundsel, presented by the wives of the policemen; the Duchess's cousin, the chatty old Viscount, and his sweet young wife; the stout old Marquis who (as every lady knows) is also admiral of the Regent's Canal, and his six old-maid daughters, who all arrived in bath chairs. The general was there, as a matter of course, with all his medals beautifully polished, and his pockets full of Pontefract cakes and peardrops to throw to the children. At least twelve bishops were present, besides the vicar and his eight kind curates, who made themselves extremely pleasant to every one.

All the mothers and fathers of the neighbourhood were present, and minders were continually arriving

ALWAYS INVENTING NEW WAYS OF MINDING

to compete for the prizes. There were at least one hundred policemen to keep order, and the music was provided by the band of the militia, lent for this occasion by the kind-hearted general. Each member of the band performed on a separate harmonium borrowed from the vicar. Refreshments also could be had by every one who could prove that he or she was hungry.

The first event was the egg-and-spoon race, which was decided in the following way. A well-pinched baby and a glass of milk were placed at the end of the course, and each competitor had to run to them balancing a new-laid egg on a spoon; when he had reached them, he had to beat up the egg in the glass of milk and pacify the child with the beverage. The competitor who did it in the shortest time won the prize.

Some murmurings were heard when it was announced that Bill had won by two-and-a-half minutes,

YOUNG TOOTH-CUTTERS FORGOT THEIR TROUBLES

but these were soon drowned by the cheers of the crowd and the music of the harmoniums.

The second event was the obstacle race, in which each competitor had to run with three babies in his arms along a course strewn with perambulators full of children. Over the latter he had to climb, and having placed his three babies in an empty perambulator stationed at the end of the course, wheel them back the same way and empty them into the arms of the Duke without a cry from the children.

The loud cheers of the crowd and the roar of the harmoniums this time hardly drowned the jeering of his rivals when it was proclaimed that Bill had also won this race; and when he secured the gold-mounted feeding-bottle, presented by the Duke, for minding seventeen tooth-cutters and three indigesters, and sending them all to sleep in three hours and forty-five minutes, their rage was almost beyond their control. The cheers, the hurrahs, and the clapping of hands, as well as the soothing music of the harmoniums, only made them more disagreeable and spiteful.

But far worse was to happen when Bill presently carried off the great cup for remaining shut up in a bathing-machine with twelve vaccinated children for twelve hours. Then they quite lost their tempers, and Bill very nearly lost his life. At least seven babies were hurled at him, as well as the cup and the bathing-machine, and Bill was only saved by the seven mothers of the seven hurled babies, who rushed forward to grapple with the hurlers, and carried Bill and the babies out of their reach.

This shocking disturbance caused the vicar and his eight kind curates to faint, while the Duke, who, now having lost all interest in the proceedings, was only waiting to give away the prizes, turned quite white, and at once drove off with the Duchess in his motor, and never again referred to the subject. The general stripped off his medals in despair, and gave them away to the children to cut their teeth with. The chatty old Viscount became dumb with astonishment, and the twelve bishops, with heads erect and half-closed eyes, walked off to their cathedrals. The harmoniums were all put out of tune and quite spoilt by the efforts of the bandsmen to drown the noise, and the tournament was completely broken up.

After this, as might have been foreseen, no mother would entrust the care of her children to any one but

THE ONLY MINDER OF THE DISTRICT

Bill, who became the only minder of the district. What became of the rivals no one ever knew for certain, though it has been said that they all emigrated to a desolate island in the Dead Sea, and clothed themselves in crocodile's hide with the rough and knobby side worn against the skin, sleeping at night on beds of flints with coverlets made of stinging nettles. It is also said that they nagged and threw stones at each other all through the day, and for very rage would eat nothing but thistles, uncooked and with the prickles left on, and drink nothing but cold vinegar for the rest of their wretched lives.

Another story has it that Bill's jealous rivals all

BILL THE MINDER

embarked for Mount Vesuvius, with the intention of committing suicide by plunging into the burning crater. But standing on its edge and gazing therein, they all suddenly altered their minds and walked back down the mountain side to Pompeii or Herculaneum, where they were supposed to have settled and married, and repented, let us hope, of their unkind and unreasonable behaviour.

Whether either of these stories is true or not, it is certain that the rivals disappeared altogether from the country. Unmolested, Bill now devoted all his days to minding, and Randall, Noah, Knut, Biddulph, Nero, Ratchett, Hannibal, Quentin, Chad, and his innumerable other charges never left him, but wandered with him everywhere, even in his dreams.

Such a minder was Bill!

THE·KING·OF·TROY

THE KING OF TROY

NOW it happened one morning as Bill was shepherding his little flock across the downs, whither they loved to ramble on a fine summer's day, that Hannibal, Quentin, and Boadicea came running up to him with the wonderful tidings that they had discovered a real golden crown lying on the top of a hayrick. Bill hastened to the spot, and there, sure enough, was a most beautiful crown, ornamented with what he took to be priceless

THE KING OF TROY

gems. Looking all round and seeing no one to whom it might belong, he climbed the rick and attempted to remove the treasure. But, try as he would, it still resisted his efforts, until at last, with one mighty wrench, he seemed to elicit a groan from the depths of the rick, and presently the crown arose apparently of its own accord and disclosed the head of an aged man firmly fixed therein. Soon his neck, then his shoulders appeared, as gradually the old fellow lifted himself from his place of hiding and climbed down the sides of the rick and stood trembling in the midst of the children, who now wonderingly gathered round him.

Having recovered from his agitation, and being greatly encouraged by Bill's kindly inquiries and genial manners, the royal old boy proceeded to account for his strange appearance on the downs.

'Prepare yourselves, you bantlings, and you, their noble curator, for the most astounding revelations; and those of you who are nerveful or softish in any way, hide your chubby heads in this old rick, that no word of my story of woes may enter your ears and so curdle your simple minds.'

At this young Chad and some of the others set up a terrible hullabaloo, but Bill soon comforted them, and then, seated in a circle on the grass around the old fellow, they made themselves comfortable and prepared to listen to his story.

'Are you all fit?' demanded the old gent. 'Yes,' shouted Bill and his charges in reply.

THE KING OF TROY

HE CLIMBED THE RICK

'Well, here goes then.' And he commenced his tale in the following way :—

'I am that King of Troy who ruled over his subjects with such wisdom and justice that the greatest happiness prevailed amongst them!'

'We've heard that before,' murmured Chad, but ignoring the interruption, the King of Troy continued his story :—

'Safely protected from baseness of every description, from robbery, from the ill effects of envy, and from unworthy tricksters of every colour, by the stern, yet just rule under which they happily lived, the Trojans throve and pursued their various trades with unvarying success. All amassed a considerable fortune, and as their wealth increased, so did their pride in the beloved city of their birth. All contributed most willingly to the upkeep of their sovereign, and the ever-increasing state which I was expected to

THE KING OF TROY

hold was paid for down to the last farthing by the noble fellows.

'The well-meaning creatures at length gave no rest to their poor old king, and as their prosperity grew, they raised him to a more and more exalted, and at the same time increasingly uncomfortable, position above them. Heavier and heavier grew the robes of state to suit the swelling dignity of the city: more and more overloaded with gold, with jewels, with filigree silver and enamelled bronze became the crown, until so ponderous had grown the regalia that I could hardly support it. But no pity had the gallant lads. Mistaking the signs of my gradually drooping spirits for the signs of undue modesty, they slapped me on the back again and again, and with joyful shouts endeavoured to instil into my dejected soul some of their own abundant ardour.

'With my own personal dignity, the number of ceremonials and functions I was expected to endure also increased. Town hall after town hall was built, and bazaars without end were held especially to be opened by myself. But in time even this doubtful relaxation ceased, and so high did my subjects raise me that few of them dared to approach me, and then only on bended knees. As for speaking familiarly with me, none had the temerity to attempt it. Perpetual state I was now compelled to keep, and never for an instant permitted to leave my throne or doff my royal robes, except for one short hour in the

THE KING OF TROY

morning to perform ablutions in the regal tub, and even then I was not allowed to remove my crown. Seated on my throne from morning until night, overburdened by the weight of my crown and the heavily brocaded and bejewelled robes, I felt as lonely as a stranded limpet in the middle of the Sahara desert.

'At last things came to such a pass, that, except perhaps to bring me food or drink, not one of my subjects would dare to draw nearer than to the outer door of my ante-room, and even there they would fall upon their faces and grovel in the dust and quake, so that the very clicking of their bones could be distinctly heard from my place upon the throne, as they trembled in every joint.

'Ah, how I missed the old days,—the cheerful cup of tea, the pipe of baccy and the homely game of dominoes with that primest of all Prime Ministers. How gladly would I have snatched from the royal board the dainties now prepared for me,—the asparagus truffles, the prawn cutlets, the anchovy jelly, and suchlike, and hurled from me the trivial and shimmering mass, tweaking my old rascal of a waiter by the nose, and calling for a hunk of bread and some cheese. Even my sparkling and frolicsome old chum, the Prime Minister, had seemingly quite forgotten our loyal chumship and never appeared before me now except upon his hands and knees and with his head bent low to the ground. And what of my old friend the Secretary of State? Where were his

THE KING OF TROY

HE COMMENCED HIS TALE

gibes, his playful fancies, his quirks and rare conceits, the droll! Alas, only rarely now could I glimpse the rogue, and with real sorrow did I see his erstwhile bonny and jovial old face distorted by expressions of the most abject servility. And that respectful mute, the Minister of Education, does he dream that I forget his winsome pranks and jokes? Does he imagine for a moment that those glorious evenings, when the four of us used to meet and gladden the very stars by the sounds of our joviality, were nothing to me? Alas, in my solitude what would have befallen me but for those sweet memories!

'One evening the Prime Minister appeared on his hands and knees at the door of the throne-room, bearing on a little plate upon his back the slight supper that was served to me in this strange manner every evening. With drooping head, and visibly

THE KING OF TROY

quaking with awe, he gradually crawled near, and when at the foot of the throne placed the supper (a mere anchovy truffle on toast) before me and fell flat on his face, writhing at my feet.

'Who can describe my feelings as I bent over him and witnessed this degradation, this prostration before me, of one who had revelled with me, who had slapped me on the back in pure amity, and who, in days of yore, had gambolled, frisked, and carolled the most enchanting glees with me. A great hot tear fell from my left eye as I gazed, and the startled wretch leapt to his feet as it splashed upon his bald crown and trickled down its glossy sides, leaving a red and glowing spot where it had fallen. No words of mine could describe the misery expressed on the face of the unhappy man as he took one hasty glance at me, full of the deepest meaning, and rushed from the room weeping bitterly. Alas! he, too, remembered.

'No heart had I now for the anchovy truffle, nor indeed for the toast, both of which I tossed lightly from me. I gave up my mind to most melancholy reflections. Night drew on, and one by one I could hear the ministers and domestics creeping up stealthily to bed, and at nine o'clock all the electric lights in the palace were switched off, and I was left in total darkness and in solitude. Still I brooded on my throne, unable to sleep for the weight of my robes and for the sad thoughts that passed through my mind, and mechanically counted the hours as they stole slowly by.

THE KING OF TROY

'At length the clock in the hall downstairs struck eleven, and as the last beat echoed through the empty rooms, a light appeared underneath the door opposite the throne. Little heed did I give to this at first, imagining that one of the ministers, on retiring, had omitted to remove his boots and leave them in the hall, and was now returning to place them there. The light, however, remained, and to my increasing wonderment some one tried the handle of the door, which was then opened very cautiously and in there crept, on hands and knees, my old friend the Prime Minister. As soon as he was well within the room and had quietly closed the door, he leapt to his feet and executed the most astonishing capers that were ever danced. With the liveliest satisfaction expressed all over his mobile features, he pirouetted round the room with the greatest animation, and daringly accomplished the giddiest somersaults that were ever turned. At last, nearly exhausted with this vigorous performance, he ran up to the throne, grasped me by the hand, which he wrung most heartily, and for all the world was his good old self again.

'He now bade me follow him, and in utter silence we both crept out of the throne-room, through the ante-room, down the stairs, across the hall, and out by the front door into the garden.

'We now traversed the terrace and crossed the tennis lawn, and stepping gently across the Rhododendron beds, scrambled as carefully as possible over the

THE KING OF TROY

barbed-wire fence and found ourselves in the kitchen garden. Passing through innumerable beds of cabbages, beetroots, turnips, brussels sprouts, and broccoli, we at last stood in front of an old broken-down hen-house. The Minister knocked very gently three distinct times and gave a low musical call, which was immediately answered from within. The door now opened just sufficiently to admit one person at a time, and the Prime Minister crept in, dragging me after him, and then closing the door as quickly and as quietly as possible.

'You may imagine my surprise when I discovered my two other old cronies seated amongst the hay newly strewn on the floor, the fat old roosters chortling wisely the while on their perches in the roof of the shed. Two or three candles, that were glued with their own fat on the stakes that were driven securely into the ground, together with an old stable lantern suspended from the roof, served to light up the interior. A squat and homely kettle was simmering cheerily in front of some glowing embers in the centre of the floor awaiting the brewing of a stout cup of tea, and the dominoes were all ready for a rattling game as of old.

'Nothing could exceed the joy of the dear old boys, as they gripped me by the hand and punched me first on the chest and again on the back from pure joy, forgetting all the awe with which they had regarded me for so long since, and only remembering the many happy times we had spent together in days of yore,—

THE KING OF TROY

those far-off happy days, before I had been so terribly, so uncomfortably exalted by my subjects.

'As soon as I had made myself pretty comfortable, the Minister of Education reached up, and taking one of the old chickens from its perch, quickly killed it, plucked it and trussed it, and then, suspending it over the embers by a piece of string from the roof, turned it round and round gently until it was done to a T.

'What a time we had in that old shed to be sure. After demolishing the chicken we played the most exciting games of dominoes until we were tired of them, then cats' cradles, then honey-pots, and then touch wood. And what could have been more refreshing than those cups of tea! And what more invigorating than the Pontefract cakes, the slabs of cocoa-nut ice, and sheets of almond hard-bake that we crunched between the games! And the songs and choruses with which we shook the crazy old henhouse to its rotting foundations! My word! How we trolled them out!

'When our joy was at its height, and we were carolling the inimitable chorus of that more than glorious old song of the country-side, "Waiting for the Guinea Fowl," we were suddenly reminded of the approach of day by the loud crowing of the old cock over our heads, and peeping at once out of the door we perceived that already the dawn had advanced and lightened the eastern sky.

'Without a moment's hesitation, the guttering

THE KING OF TROY

WHAT A TIME WE HAD

candles were extinguished, and I was hurried back to the palace. But only just in time, for as I mounted the steps of my throne I could hear the lazy steps of the boot-boy as he unwillingly crawled downstairs to his work.

THE KING OF TROY

'In the course of the day the Egg Counter to the Royal Household was dragged grovelling before me, complaining that the foxes had stolen one of the chickens under his care. I ordered the treasurer to disburse 9d. for a trap and dismissed the grinning churl, who little guessed the breed of foxes which had made away with his bird.

'Night after night the four of us, unsuspected of any, now sought the hen-house, and forgot the harassing troubles of state in the pure joys of friendship. After killing, roasting, and supping off one of the birds as on our first meeting, we abandoned ourselves to the heartiest revelry, only to be awakened to the cold everyday world by the crowing of the old bantam.

'During the daytime my friends resumed their deferential and almost servile demeanour, and nothing remained to remind me of the revels of the night before but the troubles of the Egg Counter, who now came to me every day with a fresh complaint that yet another of his birds had disappeared.

'And now begins the narration of the most terrible of all my trials. One night—how well can I remember it, it was on the eve of that very day when the mighty King of the Persians and all his court were coming to spend the week-end with us, in order to celebrate my sixty-fifth birthday—we met as usual in the hen-house, and discovered to our dismay that we had demolished all the fowls with the exception of the old cock. After some discussion, and regardless

27

THE KING OF TROY

of consequences, we decided to treat him as we had already treated his brothers and sisters, and in a very little time nothing was left of the tough old biped but bones, beak and feathers. Heedless of the morrow, we now gave ourselves up to the wildest enjoyment. Discarding such simple games as dominoes and honey-pots, we now indulged in the more thrilling joys of leap-frog, Hunt the Stag, Red Rover, Robbers and Thieves, and you would not believe me were I to tell you the amount of toffee, brandy-snaps, bull's eyes, and Edinburgh rock that we absorbed in the course of this agreeable evening.

'Enlivened, no doubt, by the thought that to-morrow was my birthday, my excitement was intense, and communicating itself to my prankful cronies, it electrified their old bones in the most amazing manner.

'How long we should have kept it up, it is, of course, impossible for me to say, but we were suddenly brought to a standstill by a loud knocking on the door of the shed and the sound of a great concourse of people on the other side. On opening the door I nearly fainted in my horror, for whom should I behold but the King of Persia and all his court, and as far as the eye could reach the faces of the Trojans all lit up by the morning sun, staring intently at the shed. Alas, we had eaten the old cock, our only timepiece, many hours ago, and without our knowledge the day had dawned and grown to midday.

THE KING OF TROY

'Who shall describe my profound mortification, as I observed the look of sorrow on the King of Persia's noble countenance, or the distress with which I viewed the agonised disappointment of my subjects as they beheld their king, whom they one and all delighted to honour, playing leap-frog in a hen-house.

'It appeared that on the arrival of the King of Persia, they had all proceeded in lordly procession with bands playing and flags flying to the throne-room, and not finding me there they had hunted everywhere for me, high and low, until at last, guided by the sounds of revelry in the hen-house, they discovered my wretched self in the ignominious position I have already described.

'I was now seized by two of the Persian guards at the command of their monarch and marched off to the Palace, a lane being opened for me through the crowds of my silent and sorrowing subjects.

'A council was very hurriedly called together, at which it was decided that I should be banished for ever from the city of Troy for so demeaning the exalted position to which I had been elevated, by my frolics in the hen-house, and that henceforth the King of Persia should reign in my stead.

'Stripping my royal robes from me (they were compelled to leave my crown on, for it was so firmly fixed that it would not come off, try as they would), they now bandaged my eyes, and, with the only baggage I was allowed to take, tied up in an old

THE KING OF TROY

patch-work quilt, they led me forth. Past crowds of my subjects, who now gave way to the most heart-felt sorrow, I was led, through the old gates of my beloved city and far out into the country. After we had travelled for about thirty miles my conductors at last removed the bandage from my eyes and left me to my despair, alone in the wilderness.

'Sinking to the ground, I wept bitterly for three-quarters of an hour, when hunger beginning to assert itself, I started upon this long journey, which has at length brought me to you.

'For many months have I travelled, often compelled to ask the way or beg assistance of the merest strangers, until at last,' concluded the old gentleman, 'as I was resting to-day in the shadow of this rick, I saw you all coming over the hill, and mistaking you for the legions of the King of Persia sent to hunt me down, I hid myself in the top of the rick.'

Bill and all his charges were deeply moved at so harrowing a tale, and willingly proffered any assistance they were capable of rendering to the unhappy old boy.

The King of Troy, now assured of the good faith of his new friends, unfolded to them a scheme he had formed to raise an army and to march on Troy, and so recover, if possible, his lost power. Bill at once offered his services and was created commander-in-chief on the spot, and calling for volunteers, was answered by one great shout of joy from all his

The King of Troy compelled to ask his way

THE KING OF TROY

charges, every one of whom enlisted there and then in the new army of the King of Troy.

Chad, Hannibal, Randall, Noah, Ratchett, Nero, Biddulph, and Knut were each promoted to the rank of officers as a matter of course, while the gentle Boadicea was deputed to look after the old King, whose comfort was now her greatest aim in life.

THE ANCIENT MARINER

THE ANCIENT MARINER

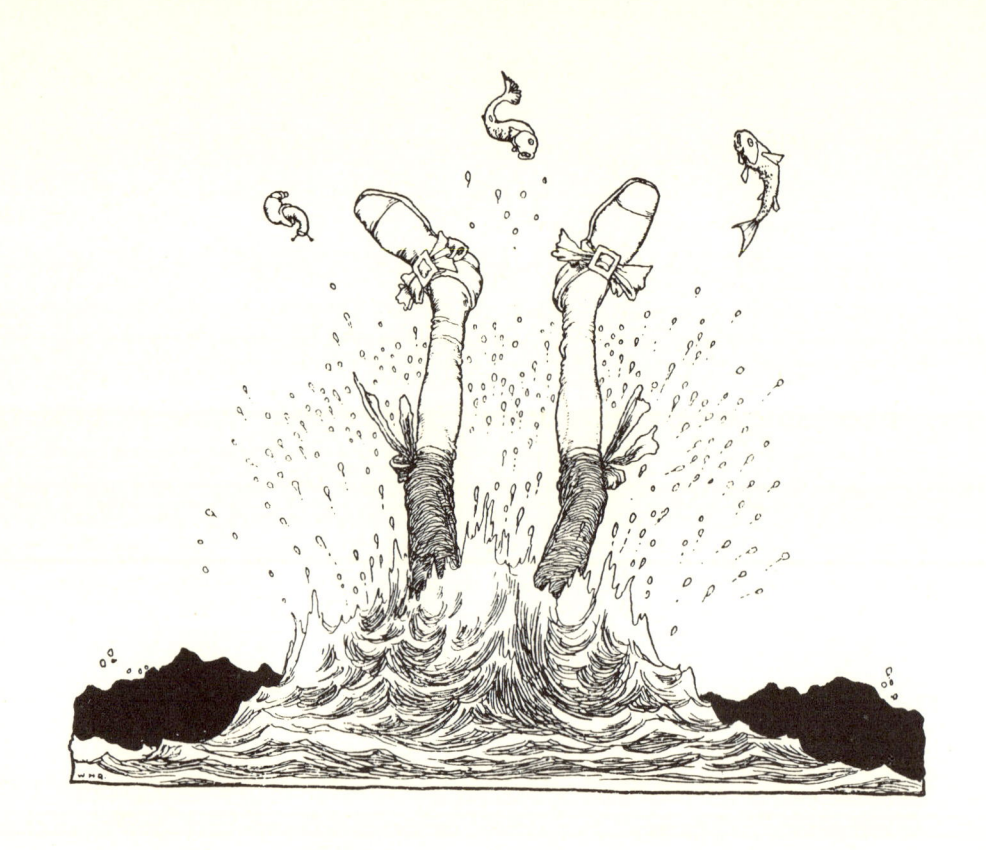

THE next thing to be done was certainly to make the old King comfortable, so Bill took him home, and the good Chloe dosed him well with hot gruel, and made him put his feet in hot water, and sent him to bed. After remaining snugly tucked up for a few days, the cheerful old soul was ready and eager to start with his new army for Troy.

In the meantime Bill, with the assistance of Crispin, had constructed a wonderful perambulator,

THE ANCIENT MARINER

in which the King could be conveyed with his luggage and such comforts as would be necessary for the old man during his progress.

Having secured the permission of Crispin and Chloe, and of the other parents concerned (most of whom seemed only too glad to get rid of the lot), Bill, the King, and all the gallant young soldiers started on their adventurous journey. Loud were the shouts of admiration as the brave creatures marched down the village street; and at last, when they had entirely disappeared, the place seemed suddenly so quiet and dull that all retired to their bedrooms and gave way to tears.

However, our duty is to follow the young braves. Having marched along the road across the Downs for some distance, they met the strangest couple,—a kind-looking old gentleman who, to judge from his appearance, had spent the greater part of his life upon the ocean, carrying in his arms, carefully and tenderly as though he were a frail young baby, another man, with the saddest and most thoughtful face that you ever beheld. Such touching kindness deeply affected all who witnessed it, and Bill at once greeted the good gentleman, and begged of him to account to them for his very strange appearance on the country road.

'Sirs,' said the Ancient Mariner, as he placed his burden lovingly on the ground, 'my name is Jack, Plain Jack, and I am the ninth mate of the Swedish ship *Turnip*, a brig-rigged barquentine, that sailed

THE ANCIENT MARINER

from Cherry Garden Pier for Margate with a cargo of camels, in the year 1840, and has never since been heard of.

'Though a born sailor, I succeeded my father in what was one of the best corn-chandler's businesses in that part of Barking. By my industry and thrift I, in time, so bettered my position and improved my business that I felt fully entitled to settle down and enter into the state of matrimony. For some years I had had my eye on the enchanting Jane Osbaldistone de Trevor, whose father kept a large brill farm by Barking Creek,—in fact, the largest of the many brill farms that used, in those days, to line the river from Limehouse Reach to Cherry Garden Pier.

'His wealth and importance did not deter me from aspiring to the hand of his fascinating daughter; and why should they have done so? Was not I in the very promising position of owning the largest corn-chandler's store, from Wapping Old Stairs even as far down as Barking Creek? And then, again, was not I as well born as he, for did not my ancestors chandle corn in Barking long before the De Trevors had crossed the Channel, when they may, indeed, have earned a precarious livelihood by letting bathing-machines on the beach at Boulogne?

'Nevertheless, on my broaching the subject to the old gentleman, he threw every conceivable obstacle in my way, and made conditions that were wellnigh impossible of being carried out. "If," said he, "you

THE ANCIENT MARINER

can bring to me, within the next few years, some object more wonderful than anything in the Bethnal Green Museum,—some object beside which St. Paul's Cathedral, the Monument, the Tower of London, or the Tower Bridge will be as uninteresting as an old one-bladed pocket-knife,—then you shall marry my daughter, but not otherwise"; and he chuckled to himself, knowing only too well that he had wellnigh dashed my hopes for ever.

'But, after all, little did he know Plain Jack. Disappointed, but with some hope yet of claiming the lovely Jane, I sold my business for a considerable sum of money, which I took with me in my sea-chest, and signed on as Cabin Boy aboard the Swedish ship, *Turnip*, fully determined to travel all over the world, if necessary, in order to fulfil the conditions imposed upon me by the irritating old gentleman.

'Foreseeing well how useful my superior officers might be to me in my quest, I resolved, as far as possible to deserve their good-will, and I behaved with such exemplary conduct that before we had passed Greenwich Hospital I was promoted to the rank of twelfth mate.

'Still persevering in my good intentions, I performed many little acts of kindness, such as brewing the captain a cup of tea when he least expected it, and handing round to the officers and crew bars of colt's-foot rock, a supply of which I took good care to bring with me. I repeat, so continually attentive was I, that,

THE ANCIENT MARINER

before we had passed the Nore, I was promoted to the rank of eleventh mate.

'Off Herne Bay, I was still further able to gratify the captain and officers by pointing out to them the various public buildings and places of interest, which I had visited only last year during a delightful week-end trip. So delighted were they all that, before sighting Margate, I was promoted to the rank of tenth mate.

'On arriving at Margate, numerous merchants came along the jetty in bath-chairs to examine our cargo. None, however, wanted to buy camels; all wanted donkeys for the sands. In spite of the captain's argument, that camels were much more used to sand than donkeys, having spent the best part of their lives on the sands of the desert, the merchants were obdurate, and we had to sail away again with our camels. We also now carried with us a shipload of Carraway Comfits, which we had purchased at Margate, hoping to be able to dispose of them at some port, and so compensate ourselves for the loss of business at Margate.

'For many days we sailed on and on, out through the Yarmouth Roads into the Persian Gulf, one incident alone standing out vividly in my memory during this part of the voyage. It was the dog-watch, on a lovely summer evening; we were making little way, just sufficient to enliven the whitebait that leapt and prattled round our prow, or disturb a lazy brill that dozed upon our course. Here and there the

THE ANCIENT MARINER

I SIGN ON AS CABIN BOY

spotted tunny would leap several yards from the sea, to descend again with a mighty smack upon the waters. From afar, borne upon the gentle breeze, came the low grizzle of the sperm-whale as it herded its young, or the thud of the mighty sword-fish, as it drove home the deadly weapon with which Nature, knowing its own ends, has provided him; while, mellowed by even greater distance, the high-pitched yell of the land-cod and the shriek of its maddened prey, could now and again be heard. I was lazily reclining among the peak halyards, whittling out a mermaid's head from a piece of hard-boiled gannet's egg, which I intended to send to Jane, should a passing vessel give me such an opportunity. Full of peace, and imbued with the calm that pervaded the sea and the sky, I was hardly prepared for the shock in store for me. Suddenly, without any warning, I was jerked from my position among the halyards, and flung head-first into the sea. Down, and down I went, until, nearly exhausted, I made one great effort to come to the surface. When at last I reached it, I found that from some unknown cause the ship had been tilted nearly on to its side, and thus had sent me almost to the bottom of the sea.

'To climb on deck and ascertain the cause of the disaster was the work of a moment. It transpired that the cargo of carraway comfits had got shifted and was mixed up with the camels. The captain was asleep at the time, and every one else seemed to lose his wits, so I at once took the matter into my own hands, and descended into the hold with twelve picked men.

'The plight of the camels was sad indeed to see. Some were fearfully chafed with the comfits, thus proving with what force the latter must have been showered upon them by the shifting of the cargo. Fortunately, however, although it was very black in the ship's hold, the camels were easily distinguished from the comfits, and it was only a work of patience and a little time to sift them and so right the ship again.

THE ANCIENT MARINER

'When the captain awakened and learnt how I had saved the ship, his gratitude knew no bounds, and he still further promoted me by making me his ninth mate.

'For years we sailed from port to port, taking in one cargo here, another there, occasionally with some advantage to ourselves, but more often with none at all, and never with any good fortune attending me in my quest. When we were about thirty days' sail out from Guatemala, and, as far as I could tell, in latitude 195 and longitude 350 (that is, about 60 degrees east of the Equator), we encountered a storm which brought me to the successful accomplishment of my quest. It was four bells and my watch below, so I had gone aloft in the mizzen shrouds, and with my feet resting idly on the top-gallant backstay, holding securely to the weather topsail reeftackle, I munched a tunny sandwich, a few of which I had prevailed upon the steward to cut for me. Under a clear sky, we were making roughly, I should say, about 335 knots, and it was already blowing half a gale; a choppy sea was running, yet, except for the clots of spindrift, that now and again hurtled against the mast, there was no real promise of the storm to come; so I went on with my sandwiches.

'We were now sailing close-hauled under double-reefed main storm topsails and fore and aft main staysails, keeping a good course and shipping very little water, when, suddenly, I beheld on the horizon,

THE ANCIENT MARINER

I WENT ON WITH MY SANDWICHES

well to windward, a little cloud no larger than a tomato,—the English tomato, I mean, not the foreign species, though it rapidly attained that size. It grew larger and larger until it was quite the size of a full-grown vegetable marrow; yet, little recking that it contained the seeds of the terrible tempest that was so soon to overwhelm us, I still went on with my sandwiches.

'Presently the gale increased, and the seas swelled

THE ANCIENT MARINER

up to the size of Ludgate Hill. Whole shoals of the passive skate arose to the surface and flopped warningly about our vessel. To leeward could be seen flocks of the wild sea shrike, whose ominous bark could be distinctly heard above the snort of the coming tempest. By now the cloud had half filled the heavens; the seas rose higher and higher; the din was terrific, as the wind tore from the sea shoal upon shoal of the shy sardine and whirled them through the air. Soon the ship was drenched in the high seas that continually broke over her and the quarts and quarts of rain that wolloped from the dense cloud now covering the whole sky and blotting out all light.

'At last came the order from the captain, who now realised the danger that threatened his vessel. "Up helm," roared he, through his speaking-trumpet, "clew up the lee braces of the topsail halyards; haul out the reef tackle and brail up the spanker." But the command came too late. The fore-topsail studding booms went by the board, carrying with them the bowsprit, the main mast, the fo'c's'le, the topgallant studding-sail halyard, and the captain's tobacco-pouch, which had been placed upon the bowsprit earlier in the afternoon. Nothing could now be seen except, here and there, the gleam on some fish as it was whirled, with the masts, men, boots, screws, sharks, thimbles, sea anemones, watchchains, ship's stores, planks, and other miscellaneous

THE ANCIENT MARINER

objects, through the sky. I had barely finished my last sandwich when, lo, everything became a blank to me and I lost all consciousness.

'How long I remained thus I cannot say, but I awakened on the sandy shore of some island, upon which I had been thrown by the force of the wind. Nothing could I see of my companions: a few planks and spars and my own wretched self were all that remained to tell the tale of the good ship *Turnip*.

'The wind had dropped, and it was a beautiful morning, not a trace of the storm remaining, only here and there the panting of the crayfish, as they nestled behind the rocks, or the gasping of the oysters telling of the strain they had undergone. I gazed along the shore in each direction, hoping to discover a bathing-machine, and so satisfy myself that the island was inhabited. Nothing was in sight, however, so I lay down again and dozed. When I awoke once more it was high noon, and the vertical rays of the sun warned me that it was time to take shelter. I raised myself on one arm with this intention, when I became aware of a strange figure, dressed in a long robe and with a great turban, who was seated on a rock near by, gazing out to sea.

'I got to my feet with considerable difficulty as I was faint with hunger and stiff in the limbs, and was about to approach the object, when I discovered two

THE ANCIENT MARINER

more figures, who evidently had the same intention. Seemingly they did not wish to be observed by the singular creature I have already described, for they were stealthily approaching him from behind, creeping from rock to rock. I at once stooped down behind a great star-fish, determined to watch unobserved.

'I now noticed that both were savages, and that one of them held close to his body an old, rusty kitchen-range; while the other carried, in one hand, a basket of coals, and with the other supported a huge, iron sauce-pan across his shoulders. Nearer and nearer drew the cannibals (as I soon guessed them to be) to their intended victim, who, however, either because he did not hear them, or did not dread them, took no notice at all. Presently they were crouching down behind him, and he was still apparently unconscious of their presence. Then, with a wild whoop they leapt into the air, and dropped on the ground in front of him. Even now the amazing creature took no notice of the cannibals or their antics, as they danced and yelled around him. Soon realising that there was something very unusual in his reception of them, they stared in awe and amazement at him for some time, and then fled in terror, leaving the saucepan, the kitchen-range and the other cooking utensils behind them.

'They ran along the sands, and dropped behind a rock at a great distance away, where they remained

THE ANCIENT MARINER

completely hidden for some long time. Presently, however, one black head appeared for an instant above the rock, and gazed in the direction of the thoughtful creature by the sea. This head was very quickly withdrawn from view and another popped up,—only to disappear as quickly. Then the first appeared again, and so on. This continued until they had regained a little of their nerve, when I could see them once more crawling back to the abstracted figure on the shore. Again they drew very close to him, and now that they had sufficiently mastered their fears, they approached and examined him very closely, and proceeded at once to prepare their evening meal. First of all they lit the fire, then they carefully placed their unresisting victim in the saucepan, after filling it with water from the sea, and were just about to lift it on to the range when I lost all patience, and shouted from my hiding-place, "Hold!" so many times in quick succession, and each time in a different tone of voice, that the cannibals must have thought there were at least thirty men or more in hiding. At any rate, they fled in the most abject terror, never to return.

'Giving them good time to disappear, I now emerged from my hiding-place and approached the absent-minded creature, gently lifting him from the saucepan, in which I found him still sitting and gazing out to sea. Gathering together many sea-urchins, rock-beetles, and branches of a succulent sea-weed, with

THE ANCIENT MARINER

FOR YEARS WE SAILED

which the beach had been strewn by the recent storm, I prepared an exquisite stew, and made a very hearty meal. I was also able to induce my companion to take some, without, however, succeeding in breaking his train of thought.

'For many months no other friend had I than this preoccupied curiosity, who seemed quite unable to give me any clue as to who he was or whence he came. Perhaps he had been shipwrecked there in childhood —who knows?—and wandered there ever since, the wonder of every limpet or lugworm that squirmed upon those shores, or the sport of every mer-kid that flipped a fin in those unknown waters.

THE ANCIENT MARINER

'To cut a long story short, I soon realised that here was the object I was in search of, and that if this dreamy creature did not sufficiently astonish old De Trevor, and compel him to consent to my marrying his daughter, nothing on this earth would do the deed, so I resolved to leave the island with my treasure as soon as I could make it possible to do so. I set about making a raft, which I quickly succeeded in completing, having since my childhood had a great knack at the making of rafts, and, without undue delay, I embarked with my prize, provisioned with as many shell-fish and branches of the succulent sea-weed as the raft would carry.

'After some few months, and just as we had finished our last limpet, we had the good fortune to be picked up by a tramp-steamer, bound for Saskatchewan from Mombasa, with a cargo of periwinkles. The captain was such a kind-hearted man that, on hearing my story he decided to go out of his course, and land us at Cherry Garden Pier; and so, my good friends, after sixty years' sailing all over the globe, I arrived home again, a poorer but a kinder man.

'You may be sure that I lost no time in seeking out Jane herself, with every hope of at last being able to claim her hand, but alas! gentlemen,' said the Ancient Mariner, with a large, salt tear about to fall from each eye, and as he once more tenderly lifted his burden, 'I was to find that Jane had become a very, very old woman, with many little grandchildren of

The sport of every mer-kid

THE ANCIENT MARINER

her own, and that she had entirely forgotten my existence. She had me turned away from her doorstep as a raving madman, even with my interesting, absent-minded, and inseparable companion.

'Thus, Good Sirs, I have to start life anew, and if my great experience should be of any service to you, believe me, it is yours to command'

THE ANCIENT MARINER

THE TRIPLETS

THE TRIPLETS

RIGHT gladly were the services of the plucky old salt accepted by the gallant little band, and taking it in turns to relieve him of his burden, they jovially marched along. The way was enlivened by many a good chorus, until the old King complained of a headache, when every one had to be quiet and talk only in quite a low tone, while Boadicea soothed the old fidget, and lulled him to sleep, by removing his crown and gently stroking the top of his head with a mint leaf, rolled into a little ball, and fastened to the end of a stem of sweet-briar. He awakened shortly after tea, very much refreshed for his nap, and every one grew merry again.

He now, however, considerably delayed the progress

THE TRIPLETS

of the expedition by insisting on running after butterflies, and trying to catch them in his crown. Though anxious enough to continue their journey, all the army awaited with great patience the pleasure of the old sportsman. At length Knut, who had been eagerly watching the King for some time, as he frisked about the fields after the brightly-coloured insects, could not restrain himself from doing likewise. Now Hannibal joined in the sport, then Quentin, then Noah, then Ratchett, and, so exciting did the chase become, soon all the force were frantically running about the fields with the lively monarch, while Boadicea remained by the carriage and darned his old stockings.

At last the King grew tired, and they all came back to the road and resumed their march. The tiresome sovereign now insisted on the Ancient Mariner removing his burden to the rear, complaining that the absent-minded creature would stare at him, and that he did not wish to be gazed at or wondered at. 'Time enough for that,' said he, 'when I'm on my throne again.' Having effected this change in the order of the procession, they now marched on without further interruption from the King.

Towards nightfall they drew near to the sea, on the shores of which they hoped to spend the night. Bill being, as usual, a little in advance of the others, was the first to descend to the sands, seated on which he discovered, to his great astonishment, three young children weeping bitterly, and near to them, in the

THE TRIPLETS

same state of grief, he beheld an old gentleman seated upon a rock. But what aroused his astonishment even more than their extreme wretchedness, was the fact that the three children were all exactly alike in every particular,—the same size, the same hair, the same eyes,—in fact, there was no perceptible difference of any kind between them. Now and again, one of the children would endeavour to comfort the old man, and he again would attempt to perform the like kindly office for them. Wondering what could so upset such worthy creatures, Bill approached and besought them to confide to him their troubles, that he might try to relieve them to the best of his ability. Their tears, however, effectually prevented them from replying at once to him. Giving them a little time to recover, Bill again addressed them. 'Who are you?' said he, and they all answered between their sobs, 'We are the Duchess of Blowdripping and her two sisters, Mellinid and Edil.'

'Which of you,' asked Bill, 'is the Duchess?'

'That's what we don't know,' they replied. 'We only know that she is neither Mellinid nor Edil.'

'Then who of you is Mellinid, and who Edil?' again queried the puzzled Bill.

'That's what all the trouble's about,' they tearfully rejoined. 'All we can tell you for certain is that neither of them is the Duchess,' and the poor little creatures redoubled their cries.

More puzzled than ever, and quite at a loss to find

THE TRIPLETS

ENDEAVOURING TO COMFORT THE OLD MAN

any clue to their troubles, Bill again besought them to relieve their minds by confiding in him. Then one of the little creatures stood up and, after drying her eyes, addressed Bill in the following way:—

'As you have most likely guessed, we are triplets, and were christened Blaura, Mellinid and Edil, after three great-aunts renowned for their intelligence and their many virtues. From our earliest days we were so much alike that each had to wear a different coloured hair-ribbon to distinguish her from her sisters. Blaura wore red, Mellinid blue, and Edil green. Our affectionate parents, the late Duke and Duchess of Blowdripping, died when we were barely six months old, and we were all left in charge of our uncle, the benevolent gentleman you see weeping on my left. Before the thoughtful creatures expired, feeling that their end was drawing near, they were faced with the difficult problem as to which of us should be the new Duchess; all of us, as I have said before, being of the same age. Of course, I need not tell you that it was quite out of the question we should all inherit the title; three young ladies trying to be one duchess would be absurd in the extreme. So our intelligent and resourceful mother and father decided, after much deliberation with the family solicitor, and the vicar of the parish, that Blaura should succeed to the title and all the dignities of the Duchy of Blowdripping when she arrived at the age of eight years, and that, at the same time, Mellinid should become the owner of Blowdripping Hall, with its priceless collections of pictures, old china, fossils and foreign stamps, and Edil become the possessor of the Blowdripping Park, in which the Hall is so pleasantly situated, with its herds of hedgehogs, elands and gnu. I am sure you will agree with me that no more just division of their great possessions could have been devised by the fair-minded couple. Our uncle was kindness itself, ever watching us with the affectionate care of a mother.

THE TRIPLETS

He was always at hand to look to our comforts, and to see that no danger drew nigh, whether we were bathing in the marble fountains of the courtyard, taking the air in the park, or sleeping in our tastefully-decorated bedroom.

'One beautiful summer's afternoon, when we were about one year old, we had been taken on to the verandah to enjoy our afternoon nap, in order that we might have advantage of the delightful breeze that blew across the woods from the sea. As usual our uncle was near by, and so soothing was the air that, unable to resist its drowsy influence, he, too, soon dozed off. Unfortunately we awakened before our unconscious nurse, and immediately rolled out of our cradles, and crawled along the pavement of the verandah. Great sport we had, I have no doubt, as children will, and certain it is that, attracted by their brilliant colours, we lost no time in removing from each other's heads our distinguishing ribbons, and speedily mixing them up. However, at length, and too late, our baby laughter awakened the old gentleman from his sleep. Too great for words was the astonishment of the unhappy man when he beheld us all shuffled up and mixed in this deplorable way upon the pavement. Bitterly he accused himself of wicked negligence for allowing such a thing to happen, for so alike were we without our distinguishing ribbons, that he could never hope to know one from the other again. He thought, and thought, and thought for the whole afternoon, but

THE TRIPLETS

WE GREW UP IN COMPARATIVE HAPPINESS

at the end he was no nearer discovering again which was the future Duchess, which Mellinid, and which Edil. At last, he gave it up in despair. Henceforth we were known only collectively as the future Duchess and her two sisters, but which is the Duchess, and which the two sisters, will remain for ever a mystery.

'Nevertheless, we grew up in comparative happiness until yesterday, the fateful day when we all became

He was always at hand

THE TRIPLETS

eight years of age. Before breakfast, and with all due solemnity, our faithful uncle handed over to us the control and guardianship of the Blowdripping possessions, which had been entrusted to him until we should arrive at our present age, but, alas! we could not avail ourselves of the good provision made for us by our thoughtful parents, as neither one of us knew which of us we were. The Duchess, as head of the family, could not give her consent to anything, or advance any money for the housekeeping as, for all she knew, she might be one of her own sisters, in which case she would have been touching that which did not rightly belong to her. For the same reason Mellinid, not knowing who she herself was, could not give her consent to our remaining at the Hall, and likewise Edil could not allow the magnificent house still to occupy its lovely situation in the Blowdripping Park. After talking the matter over, and over again, we have come to the conclusion that, without the permission of the proper owners, which, you will see, it is impossible for us to obtain, the only course open to us was to abandon our riches, and to leave the park and the castle for ever. Our good uncle, putting all the blame for our troubles upon his own negligence, insisted on accompanying us.'

At the conclusion of this strange story Bill was certainly aghast at the very difficult problem put before him, and quite at a loss to offer any solution. He therefore conducted the trembling triplets and their

THE TRIPLETS

grief-stricken uncle before the King, who had in the meantime arrived upon the shore. Bill explained the difficult position in which the poor young things found themselves; but, wise as he undoubtedly was, the King for some time could make nothing whatever of it. He called all his officers and soldiers round him, and they formed one great semicircle, of which he was the centre; the triplets were then placed before him, and he at once proceeded to question them.

'Have you,' said he, addressing the first triplet, 'any idea as to which of the three of you you really are?'

'None whatever,' answered the child.

He then repeated the same question to the other triplets, and received the same answer.

'Come now,' continued the King, in a cheerful voice, 'does any one of you feel at all like a duchess?'

'We don't know how a duchess should feel,' they all replied.

The King here frowned severely and ground his teeth.

'Now, one of you must be telling an untruth,' said he, 'for one of you, as you say, is the Duchess, and must know exactly how she feels, which must be how a duchess feels. Come now, which of you is she?' And the quick-tempered monarch knit his brows into the most terrible folds. 'Unless that one is one of her own sisters and not the Duchess,' he roared, 'she ought to be ashamed of her deceit, and severely

THE TRIPLETS

punished; and if, indeed, she is not the Duchess, then she ought to be punished all the same. I've half a mind to have the three of you smacked hard, that I may at least be certain of punishing the right one.'

Bill suggested timidly that perhaps this would be rather unfair, as two of them at least would be unjustly punished.

'But which two?' snapped the irritated King. 'How can any of them feel unjustly treated if she doesn't know whether she's the guilty one or not?' And he worked himself into a terrible fury, and strode up and down the sands, no one daring to approach him. Suddenly, without any warning of his intention, he ran down to the sea, and removing his shoes and stockings, cooled his temper by paddling his feet in the sea-water. In a little time he returned, his excitement much allayed, and soon the cries of the distracted and unhappy triplets, together with the pitiful sighs of the dejected uncle, entirely assuaged the wrath of the sympathetic, though quick-tempered, old man.

When he once more resumed his place before the three children the storm had passed, and a sweet, good-natured smile enlivened his homely old face, and charmed all beholders.

'Well, well, well,' said he, 'triplets will be triplets after all, and uncles uncles, all the world over.'

THE TRIPLETS

He at once resumed the inquiry, and placing his hand kindly on the head of the second triplet he now addressed the first in the following way:—

'Let us suppose for the moment that you happen to know which of your sisters this particular one really is, who, in that case, would the third one be, if she (the third) were not Mellinid?'

'Either Edil or the Duchess,' promptly replied the intelligent child.

'Quite right,' said the King encouragingly, 'Now as this is not so, and you certainly do not know which of your sisters this one happens to be, the reverse must be true, so that if your other sister is neither Edil nor the Duchess, who must she be?'

'Mellinid, of course,' readily answered the child, and every one applauded and wondered at the wisdom of the King.

'It only now remains,' proceeded the King, addressing the first and second triplets 'to discover which of you is Edil and which the Duchess.' Placing his hand once more upon the head of the second triplet, he again addressed the first.

'Suppose, for the sake of argument, that this sister of yours whom we now know not to be Mellinid were Mellinid and Mellinid the Duchess, in that case you would assuredly be Edil. Now as you cannot suppose this sister to be Mellinid when you know she is not, and the Duchess is the Duchess and not Mellinid, then our supposition must be wrong and the reverse

62

THE TRIPLETS

THE TRIPLETS ACCOMPANY THE ARMY

true, so that Mellinid remains Mellinid and, as we say you are not Edil, then this little girl must be she.' Then shaking the first triplet by the hand, the complacent old potentate said in conclusion:—'And you, my dear creature, are thus proved to be neither Edil nor Mellinid but Blaura, the charming Duchess of Blowdripping, to whom I offer my hearty congratulations.' The cheerful soul now embraced the three children, and when he had a hand free he slapped the old uncle, who now looked the very picture of happiness, several times upon the back.

Cheers were raised again and again at the unheard-of wisdom of the King of Troy. The old uncle completely exhausted himself by leaping high into the air over and over again, while the triplets were beyond themselves with joy at such a successful end to their troubles.

So delighted were the triplets with their new friends that, during breakfast the next morning, they announced their intention of accompanying them to

THE TRIPLETS

their journey's end, and entrusted the care of the Blowdripping estate to their old uncle until they should return. The camp packed up and when every one was ready to continue the journey, they all took an affectionate leave of the old man and marched on.

GOOD AUNT GALLADIA

GOOD AUNT GALLADIA

AT first the King seemed disposed to be not a little irritable towards the triplets, murmuring something to himself about the extra expense. A good lunch, however, soon put him to rights, and he was his old cheerful self again.

In the afternoon they met upon the road a long thin man with a grin of the greatest self-satisfaction widening his otherwise narrow face. In one hand he carried a cage containing a miserable old bird that could hardly boast an egg-cupful of feathers on its

GOOD AUNT GALLADIA

whole shrivelled body; in the other he carried a large wooden box. He very good-naturedly stood aside for the army to move on, but the King, whose curiosity had been aroused, would not allow him to be passed unquestioned, so he rang a little bell he always carried with him for the purpose, and the whole force at once stopped short. In obedience to a signal from the King, the long man stepped jauntily before him. 'Anything wrong, old chirpy?' said he, addressing the King rather rudely as some thought. 'Not with me,' the King replied with much dignity. 'My only reason for calling you before me is to learn why you are so extremely pleased with yourself. Such a secret would be of the greatest value to us all.' 'Because she's given these back to me,' answered the long fellow as he opened his box and disclosed, all neatly arranged, a beautiful collection of birds' eggs. Every kind appeared to be there, and all of the most beautiful colours imaginable.

'But who is she?' queried the King.

'Why, my good Aunt Galladia, of course, but it's too long a story to tell standing up, so let us sit down by the roadside, and you shall hear all about it.'

Every one now seated themselves on the grass by the side of the road and over a comforting cup of tea, speedily brewed by Boadicea, the long man began his story:—

'My good aunt's full name was Galladia Glowmutton, and she was the only daughter of that

GOOD AUNT GALLADIA

gallant general, Sir Francis Melville Glowmutton, who distinguished himself so greatly in the defence of his country.

'It was my good fortune to spend my earliest days in this good creature's company, she, noble soul that she was, having undertaken to look after me when my poor father and mother disappeared in a sand-storm many years before.

'The greater part of her life this good woman had devoted to brightening the declining years of her well-loved father, whose arduous life, poor man, had left him in his old age, truth to tell, rather a tiresome, and sometimes a difficult, subject to get on with. However, thanks to her devotion and patience, he led a tolerably happy life. In the course of time the old warrior died and left the sorrowing lady well provided for,—that is, over and beyond necessaries, with sufficient money to keep up appearances, and even enough for her simple pleasures and hobbies.

'For some months my good aunt could not fill the blank in her life left by the loss of her father. So much kindness, however, could not be kept back for long, and was bound in the course of time to find its object. Always with a love for every feathered creature, she at last set about gathering around her as complete a collection of them as she could obtain. Soon she had in her aviaries the most marvellous assembly of birds ever brought together even at the Zoo. There were specimens of the Paraguay gull, Borneo parrots, Australian gheck ghees, the laughing grete, Malay anchovy wren that only feeds upon anchovies (and very amusing indeed it is, too, to watch them spearing the little fish with their beaks and then trying to shake them off again), and the golden-crested mussel hawk, that swoops down from an incredible height and, snatching its prey from the rocks, again disappears in the sky. Without wearying you with a long list, nearly every known bird was represented in my aunt's collection, from the fierce saw-beaked stork of Tuscaroca to the mild and pretty little Gossawary chick.

'Much as she prized every one of her pets, she loved most of all the very rare and beautiful green-toed button crane of Baraboo. So fond was she of the stately creature, and so careful of its every comfort, that she employed a maid to wait on it alone, and a special cook to prepare its meal of Peruvian yap beans, the delicious and tender kernels of which the dainty creature was inordinately fond of,—and, indeed, they were the only food upon which it throve.

'Now, with your permission, a few words about myself. Like my aunt I, too, had birdish leanings, but unlike her in this, that instead of birds I collected birds' eggs, of which I had a vast number of every conceivable variety. Ashamed as I am to state it, little did my good Aunt Galladia know how many of the valuable specimens in my collection were taken from her aviaries. Nevertheless she viewed my

GOOD AUNT GALLADIA

specimens with growing suspicion, until at last she implicitly forbade me to collect any more. For a time I desisted, and merely contented myself with gloating over my already vast collection, but in a little while temptation became too strong for me and I resumed my pursuits.

'One afternoon about this time I had mounted a tall tree in the Glowmutton Park, intent on obtaining the contents of a nest built in its highest branches. For some time I was unable to approach the nest, but at length, by dint of much perseverance, I just managed to reach my hand over the top, and took therefrom three beautiful eggs, of a kind as yet unrepresented in my collection. So occupied was I with my prize, that I did not at first observe what was taking place beneath the tree. But on beginning to descend, I saw to my horror immediately below me, my Aunt Galladia and her pet crane seated at tea, with the crane's maid in attendance.

'Needless to say I did not continue my descent, but climbed out to the end of a branch, high over the group. I waited in dreadful suspense in the hope that my aunt would not look up, and that they would soon finish their meal and depart as quickly as they had arrived, but, alas! they were in no hurry. I trembled now so much that I could hear the leaves rustling on the branch, and whether it was that in my fear I loosened my hold, or that the branch shook so under my trembling form, or whether the sight of a

GOOD AUNT GALLADIA

I JUST MANAGED TO REACH THE EGGS

beautiful plum cake, directly over which I was poised, made me lose my nerve, I know not, but certain it is that I fell from my position right on to the table. Both my aunt and the maid fainted at once quite away, and the timid green-toed button crane of Baraboo was in such a terrible flutter that in its excitement it snapped the slender gold chain that held it and flew into the sky, where it was soon lost to view. "Now I've done it," thought I, and, no doubt, should have run away had I been able to move, but I was so bruised that I was compelled to remain among the shattered remains of the table and tea things. Presently the maid came to, and then my aunt, and nothing could exceed her rage and grief at losing her valuable pet. They took me home between them and put me to bed, and the severest punishment they could devise was to take away from me my lovely

GOOD AUNT GALLADIA

I ANGLE THE AIR

collection of eggs. "Never," shrieked my wrathful aunt, "shall you have these again until you bring back to me my beautiful crane."

'After a while I recovered, but no one dared to speak to me, and I moped about the house in solitary wretchedness without a single egg to contemplate.

'At last I could bear it no longer, and one night I left the house determined never to return again without the crane. I took with me an old perambulator, in which I had been wheeled about as a child, and

I fell from my position

GOOD AUNT GALLADIA

I ERECTED MY POLE ON THE SANDS

in this I placed six of the delicious kernels of the Peruvian yap bean, besides a hatchet and other things which I thought might be useful on my journey. I slept in the forest and, on the following morning I cut down the straightest tree I could find for my purpose, trimmed it to a fine long pole, and on the very top of this I fastened a pin, bent to the form of a fish-hook, which I now baited with one of the yap kernels.

"'If anything will attract the bird, this will,' thought I, having fastened the foot of the pole to my perambulator. I now proceeded to angle the air for the lost crane. Carefully following the direction I had observed the bird to take when it broke away from its chain, I travelled for weeks and weeks, without seeing any sign of it. In time, without even a nibble, the first kernel was dissolved and worn away by the wind and rain, and, in like manner the same fate overcame the second, with which I baited my hook; then the third, then the fourth, and then the fifth.

'Still keeping the same direction, by this time I had arrived at the very edge of the world, beyond which there is nothing but sea and sky. Believing that the poor creature had flown out over this lonely sea, and hoping that it might return when it realised that there was no land beyond, I determined to wait on the desolate shore.

'I now erected my pole on the sands, after once more baiting my hook, this time with a piece of my last kernel, having taken the precaution of cutting it into six pieces. I now waited patiently, week after week, subsisting on the oysters, the starfish, and the edible crustaceans, that wandered tamely about the shore. Months now passed by, and, one by one, the five pieces of my last yap kernel had followed the other five kernels with which I had set out from home. I am not easily beaten, however, and though many months had passed by without my meeting with any success, I would not give in, but husbanded my last piece of bait with the greatest care. I cut a chip of wood from my angling pole, and shaped it in the form

GOOD AUNT GALLADIA

ITS OLD STATELY SELF AGAIN

of a kernel of the Peruvian yap bean. This I rubbed well all over with the tiny piece of the real kernel that yet remained to me, until it assumed somewhat the colour of the original bean and, certainly, when applied to the tip of the tongue, it appeared to partake, though very slightly, it is true, of the original flavour, and with this I once more baited my hook.

'By this means I made my last piece of bean last for some years, for as soon as the artificial bean had lost its flavour, I rubbed it up again with the real one. But even this could not go on for ever, and, at last, the true piece was worn right away; so, to preserve what little flavour there yet remained of the true bean in the false bean, on which it had been so often rubbed, I soaked it for six days in a large shell of rain-water. In the meantime I cut another chip from my pole, and spent nearly six days in carving out another artificial

GOOD AUNT GALLADIA

kernel. Before baiting my hook with this, I dipped it into the fluid in which the old wooden kernel was still soaking, whence it received a very very faint suggestion of the original flavour, but so faint was this that it had to be redipped three times a day. This went on for some time, until the precious liquor began to run low, and I was compelled to dilute it still further, in the proportion of about five drops to a mussel-shellful of water, into which the wooden kernel was now dipped ten or twelve times a day.

'Well, I had been at this game, I should say, getting on for twenty years, and now resolved to have done with it, after risking all on one throw. So I dropped my wooden kernel, all rotted and weather-beaten as it was, into what little there remained over of the pure liquor, this time without diluting it at all, and then let it stew all day in the sun.

'In the evening the liquor was all evaporated, and the wooden bean seemed to the taste as though it possibly might have been in the vicinity of a real one some time before. On that evening, for the last time, I baited my hook and slept soundly at the foot of the pole.

'I was awakened next morning by the wind that had arisen during the night, and a great wrenching noise, as it tore my poor old angling-pole from its place in the sand, and carried it out to sea.

'"That settles it once and for all," thought I, much relieved, "and I'm off home," and I set about getting my things together. While I was thus engaged, it occurred to me that the old pole might be useful for fires, so I swam out for it. Already it had been blown some way out to sea, and, as the tide was against me, it was only with a very great exertion of strength that I gained at all upon it, and I was just about to give it up when I beheld, fastened to the bent pin at the end of the pole, the wretched crane. The sight lent me greater strength, and, after incredible exertions, I reached the pole almost exhausted. We were now too far from the shore to attempt to return, so I got astride the pole, and immediately proceeded to unfasten the unhappy fowl from my bent pin. At first I thought the poor thing dead, but I nursed it in my arms all through the ensuing night, and, on the following morning, happening to glance down its half-opened beak, I could just see that my wooden imitation of the kernel of the Peruvian yap bean had become lodged in its throat. This I at once removed, and, to my great joy, the dejected fowl almost immediately opened its eyes. Soon it became its old stately self again, though now I could see that the poor thing had aged very considerably since it left home.

'Well, to cut a long story short, at length the gale ceased, and we landed safely on the shore, much nearer to our home, and, after many vicissitudes and adventures, of which I shall have great pleasure in telling you at another time, we eventually arrived at Glowmutton Castle.

GOOD AUNT GALLADIA

'To my grief I learnt that my good aunt, Galladia, had died many years before of old age, and that, true to her own good-nature, her last commands were that if ever I should return with her dearly-loved fowl, my collection of eggs was to be handed back to me, and in recompense for all my privations and exertions to recover the bird, I was to have the care of it and the comfort of its society as long as it lived. So, now you see why I am so pleased with myself.'

The King and the whole army were charmed with the recital, and the long man, whose many noble qualities had already endeared him to them, was cordially invited to join the forces.

'It's all one to me, my cronies,' said the good-natured creature, and they all trudged on.

THE DOCTOR

THE DOCTOR

FOR many days they had now travelled without meeting with any adventure, when one evening they saw coming towards them a bright young lad, who was leading by the hand an exceedingly learned-looking old gentleman. Their appearance was such as to arouse the King's curiosity to such a degree that he asked the boy the time as he was passing, and then, when all stood still in the road, he led the talk from one thing to another until at last, emboldened by their friendliness, the King came to the point,

THE DOCTOR

and asked the lad who he was and whence he had come.

The two strangers then sat down at the side of the road, and the lad thus addressed the King:—

'You may not believe it, but I am the original Ptolemy Jenkinson, the only and well-beloved nephew of that great and celebrated doctor, Ebenezer Scrout, whom you now see at my side. When, a trembling orphan, I was thrown upon an unfeeling world, he alone of my numerous uncles, aunts, so-called friends and guardians, undertook to find me a comfortable and even luxurious home, and so to educate me that I might prove worthy of occupying the exalted position for which I am destined.

'Uncle Ebenezer was my mother's brother and, a true Scrout, he inherited all his good qualities from my grandfather, Phelim Scrout, the well-known turf-cutter, from whom, by the way, I inherit most of mine—but of these it does not become me to speak.

'Many people, jealous perhaps of his great fame, have ridiculed my uncle's claim to be a member of this ancient family, but to set this matter for ever at rest, I have here copied a few notes from the Scroutean genealogical tree, preserved in the archives of the family.' Ptolemy Jenkinson here took from his pocket and handed to Bill a sheet of paper upon which the following notes were written in a clear bold hand:—

THE DOCTOR

MISTS OF THE PAST

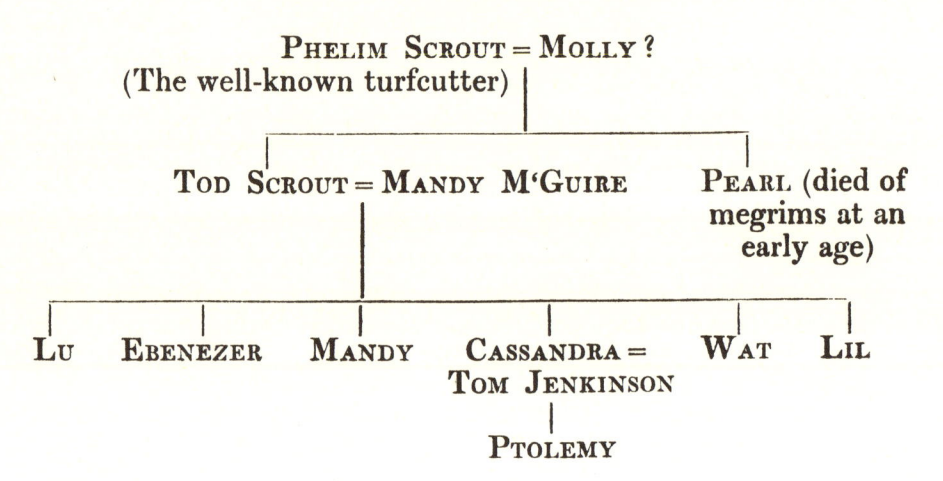

```
        PHELIM SCROUT = MOLLY?
    (The well-known turfcutter)  |
                 ┌───────────────┴──────────────┐
          TOD SCROUT = MANDY M'GUIRE       PEARL (died of
                     |                       megrims at an
                     |                         early age)
   ┌────────┬────────┼────────┬────────┬────────┐
   LU  EBENEZER   MANDY   CASSANDRA =  WAT     LIL
                          TOM JENKINSON
                               |
                            PTOLEMY
```

When these had been examined by the company, Ptolemy resumed his tale :—

'Uncle Eb, as I very soon learned to call him, was ever the victim of his own generous heart. Continually adopting people, both old and young, he was doomed to be taken advantage of by those to whom he was most kind. How well can I remember, amongst many another ungrateful adopted son, uncle, aunt or cousin, young Sigurd, the birthday-monger, who entered the family about the same time as myself. It was he who secretly wrote his name on each page of Uncle Eb's birthday-book and received a present every day from the absent-minded old gentleman until he was discovered writing his name twice on some pages and was straightway disadopted.

'Not alone to his own family circle was the doctor's

FAR SOONER HAVE THE MUMPS

THE DOCTOR

kindness confined; it extended to all with whom he came in contact. Before sending in his bills he always provided his patients with enough money to pay them, and promptly returned the cash with the receipts, deducting only one penny for the stamp in each case.

'Invariably most sympathetic with his suffering patients, he spent many years of his noble life in studying how to make his medicines as pleasant and sweet to the taste as the most delightful confections ever placed upon the Lord Mayor's table, while his greatest endeavour was always to make a period of sickness one also of pleasurable relaxation for his patients.

'In time the children went mad with excitement, and jumped for very joy on learning that they had contracted measles, and would far sooner, any day, have the mumps than a birthday every week. And oh! what thrills of joy would pass through their little frames on learning that they would have to lie up for a bilious attack and be attended by the good-natured Doctor Ebenezer Scrout, and treated with his delicious jalaps and powders.

'Unfortunately, however, so pleasant was the treatment, that the children in time were even tempted to make themselves ill on purpose, by eating as many jam puffs as they could buy with their Saturday monies, and soon nearly every child was down with a bad bilious attack, and all the schools had to be closed.

THE DOCTOR

'Even the grown-ups began to indulge in these jam puffs, buying them in large quantities and falling ill one by one, much preferring to be tucked up snugly in bed with a comfortable bilious attack and the good-natured doctor in attendance, to ordinary good health and hard work, with the many disappointments and trials of everyday life.

'First the Lord Mayor was taken bad—then the leader of the town band and all his bandsmen. Now the shopmen began to feel queer, and one by one the aldermen toddled to their beds. In time everybody was laid up, and no one was left to do the work of the town. All the shops, theatres, markets, and railway stations were closed, and the streets quite deserted except for the doctor and the puff baker, each trying to undo the work of the other.

'Hardly a sound could be heard in the streets except perhaps the clink of a spoon against a bottle from a room above, as some patient prepared his evening dose, or the shuffling footsteps of the old doctor as he went his daily round, and sometimes the loud rat-tat of the puff baker would awaken the echoes of the lonely streets as he called from door to door for orders in the morning.

'Strange grasses and sweet-scented wild flowers began to grow in the streets, and mushrooms and straggling carrots forced a way between the crevices of the pavements. Sprays of wild spinach hung from the lamp-posts, and the market-place became one

THE DOCTOR

waving jungle of broccoli. The very sparrows, deprived of their daily crumbs, grew thin and nervy with the green diet they were compelled to subsist upon. Croaking and griding, instead of chirruping musically to their young as is their wont, they so affected the good-hearted doctor that he could never pass them without some cheering word, and never could he withstand the beseeching look in their eyes. Within doors the prospect was hardly more encouraging. Strong vegetable-marrows twined their branches and their many tendrils round the table legs and the chairs; great turnips stoutened and burst upon the stairs; spring onions bristled in the corners of the Lord Mayor's dining-hall, while his grand piano was completely hidden in the gorgeous festoons of mint that, unchecked, had run a ragged riot about the place.

'At last, after two months of sickness, and despite every attention and kindness on the part of the doctor, the patients began to weary of being ill and kept to their beds for so long. The Lord Mayor was the first to arise and, although very weak in the legs, he managed to crawl to the top of the stairs, and looking down, beheld, to his dismay, the dreadful state of ruin in which everything was involved. He called for his servants as loudly as his weakness would allow him, and, obtaining no reply, he scrambled down the stairs on his hands and knees, and clamoured shrilly for a cut from the joint. As, of course, there was no one

THE PUFF BAKER

THE DOCTOR

TREATED WITH DELICIOUS JALAPS

to procure this for him nor, indeed, any joint from which to procure a cut, he boiled himself an egg, and was able to survey the scene more calmly.

'Presently the aldermen crawled down one by one, then the shopmen, then the bandsmen, and, finally, the rest of the inhabitants, disturbed by the weeping and yells of those already arisen, struggled downstairs, and in agony beheld the general devastation.

'Resolved not to touch another drop of the doctor's medicine, they satisfied the cravings of their hunger, which now began to be felt, on the wild marrows, turnips, and mushrooms that everywhere abounded, and by degrees regained a little of their former vigour.

'The Lord Mayor and aldermen, already feeling a little more comfortable, held a long council, at which it was decided that it would be less expensive to burn the old town, and to build a new one on its site, than to try and clear up the old one. It was also decided

The Lord Mayor held a long council

THE DOCTOR

AS SOME PATIENT PREPARED HIS DOSE

to arrest the unfortunate doctor, whom they all now joined in accusing as the cause of their trouble, and bring him to trial.

'In the course of time the town was rebuilt, and the doctor was the first prisoner to stand on his trial at the new Town Hall.

'On the appointed day the Hall was crammed to its utmost, as at one time the prisoner had been much loved and looked up to by his fellow-townsmen.

'When the Lord Mayor arrived in state, between two Admirals of the Fleet, and took his seat, the foreman of the jury awakened his brother-jurors, who had been dozing off, and called for three cheers for the Lord Mayor, in which everybody joined. The Lord Mayor made no reply, except to frown severely at the foreman, and proceeded at once with the business in hand. "Lock all the doors and bring in the prisoner,"

THE DOCTOR

cried he in a loud voice, after clearing his throat. The doors were instantly locked, but some confusion arose when it was discovered that they could not bring in the prisoner unless one were unlocked again. On this being very politely pointed out to the Lord Mayor (who did not seem quite to like being corrected), he altered his order, and cried out: "Bring in the prisoner, and lock all the doors." Immediately the band struck up the most martial music and the prisoner was brought in, tied tightly with twine, sealed with red sealing-wax, and guarded by a squad of infantry, who at once formed fours, and marked time for the rest of the afternoon.

'When the music had ceased, and the general excitement caused by the entrance of the prisoner had subsided, the Lord Mayor politely requested him to take a seat, which he very gladly did, on being untied by the policeman.

'Now, as every one knew that the doctor had really been the cause of all the trouble, the only point to be decided at the trial was whether he had done it intentionally or not, and the Lord Mayor addressed him accordingly, asking him if he had anything to say upon the subject. The doctor happened to be thinking of something else at the moment and, moreover, had his head turned in another direction, watching a fly on the window of the hall, so that he did not hear the question. The Lord Mayor waited about a quarter of an hour for an answer, and receiving none, he

THE DOCTOR

THE VERY SPARROWS GREW THIN

called, in an annoyed tone, for the witnesses for the prosecution.

'The principal witness for the prosecution was a Sicilian char-woman, whose evidence was translated by one of the many aldermen present to assist in case of need. It appeared that in her young days she had made the acquaintance of a young and handsome Sicilian waiter, a distant cousin, and a native of the village in which she was born. So friendly did they become in time that he had confided to her many of the secrets of his life, and, amongst others, one that had weighed very heavily upon his mind. Some time previously, when employed at a well-known refreshment hall, on the coast of Lombardy, he had waited upon a distinguished young gentleman of considerable means, and had overheard him whisper to a chance acquaintance, seated at the next table, that a friend of his, a tall dark man, had met a young lady at a whist-party, whose greatest friend had an aunt, formerly engaged to a well-meaning curate, who averred that his brother knew for certain that IT WAS DONE QUITE INTENTIONALLY BY —— Here the waiter was called away to another client, and did not hear the rest of the sentence.

'Now the Sicilian char-woman, on hearing this from her good friend, was much puzzled, and not knowing to whom the words might refer, made a mental note of it at the time. On reading of the arrest of the doctor, however, and of what he was accused, she concluded that there must be some connection between him and the man mentioned by the brother of the well-meaning curate formerly engaged to the aunt of the greatest friend of the young lady who was met at the whist party by the tall dark friend of the young gentleman of considerable means who, as you know, was waited upon by the Sicilian waiter at the well-known refreshment hall in Lombardy, so she had hastened from Sicily

THE DOCTOR

to tell her tale. At the conclusion of her evidence a murmur of admiration was heard all over the court, and the Lord Mayor was so charmed with her and the really pleasant way in which she had told her tale, that he lightly threw a half-crown to her across the hall, which she very neatly caught. She then sat down, amidst the cheers of the crowd.

'The principal witness for the defence was a young journeyman tailor, who stated that on cleaning out the pockets of an old coat which had been left at his house for repairs by a dark gentleman of mysterious appearance, he had discovered an old envelope upon which he could just trace the figures 56—6.30 A.M. The coat was never called for, and the tailor pondered over the envelope, but could make nothing of it. He showed it to every policeman of his acquaintance, but not one could unravel the mystery, and, as a last resource, he procured an introduction to the principal policeman in the British Museum Library. This great man examined the envelope very carefully, but with no result, and the only advice he could give him was to call at every house numbered 56 at 6.30 in the morning and see what would happen.

'The tailor followed this advice diligently for some time and met with many rebuffs, as he had nothing to say on the door being opened to him. At length one morning he came to an empty house numbered 56, the steps of which were littered with straw. Gazing hopelessly at this for some time, he noticed that three

THE DOCTOR

pieces pointed distinctly in one direction to the corner of the street, and you may well imagine his surprise when, on following the direction indicated by the straw, he came across this postcard.'

Ptolemy Jenkinson here handed this torn postcard to the company.

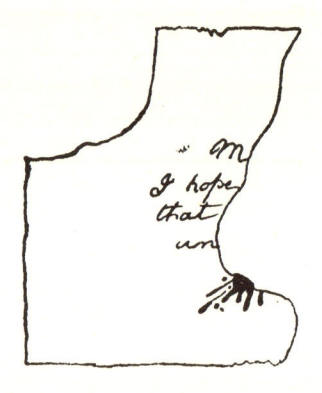

Ptolemy again proceeded with his story:—

'Now the tailor, more puzzled than ever, took the card home, and, after weeks of deep thinking, decided that the card must have been completed thus.'

Ptolemy here handed the remaining portion of card, with the tailor's suggested completion, to the company.

'You may guess the surprise of every one present when the tailor produced the completed card. The Lord Mayor gazed at it in astonishment. He turned it over and over, and suddenly noticing that there was a foreign stamp on the other side, he became more excited than ever, and asked if he might tear

THE DOCTOR

it off, as his son had rather a good collection. This the tailor readily allowed him to do, and this put the Lord Mayor in a good temper for the rest of the afternoon, and gave a more cheerful aspect to the case altogether.

'After the tailor's evidence, which, of course, proved that the doctor had not intended to bring about the harm of which he had been the unfortunate cause, there was nothing for the Lord Mayor to do but to acquit the prisoner, which he did, much to everybody's relief.

'The Lord Mayor then retired, after ordering a new suit of clothes from the journeyman tailor, and inviting the Sicilian charwoman and the other witnesses to progressive whist and to be introduced to his family.

'So, Gentlemen,' said Ptolemy in conclusion, 'my uncle and myself are quite free at last, and entirely at your service.'

THE DOCTOR

Such a valuable offer could not very well be refused, so, after explaining the object of the expedition to their new friends, the whole force moved joyfully on.

THE RESPECTABLE GENTLEMAN

AND THE BOY SCOUT

THE RESPECTABLE GENTLE-MAN AND THE BOY SCOUT

IN due time the gallant army arrived at the little town of Killgruel, a very respectable place indeed, at which they spent the pleasantest of week-ends, entertained at 'At Homes,' soirées, and receptions, to any number of which every member of the expedition was invited during their brief stay. Bill and the King were the guests of the very respectable and Right Honourable Hesketh Fitzgreynib, the Mayor of Killgruel, who entertained them with the extremest gentility imaginable. So respectable and

THE RESPECTABLE GENTLEMAN

genteel was their host, that it had been said of him that never had he been known to don the same suit twice, having at the very least a new one every day; nor had he ever been seen to remove his lavender gloves even at meal times. It was also reported that, not content with bowing most politely to every one he met in the street, he behaved in a like genteel manner to all the pillar-boxes and lamp-posts that he passed upon his way, and that he always walked sideways down the street with his back to the wall, in order that he should not be compelled to turn it upon the passers-by. Whether these reports are true or not, it is certain that he was the most gentlemanly gentleman in all Killgruel, a town which could boast more elegant and refined people than any other town in the whole world.

He was indeed the pride of Killgruel, and so respected by his fellow-townsmen, who valued him greatly for his exceptional gentlemanliness, that he was not allowed to soil his hands by so much as a stroke of work, but only to be respectable from morning to night. An intelligent boy scout was employed to look after him, and even to think for him, with orders never on any account to leave him, so that in time this respectable gentleman became very respectable indeed, and relying for almost everything on the intelligence and affection of the boy scout, who now performed for him even his duties as Mayor of Killgruel, the good man was enabled to devote his

THE RESPECTABLE GENTLEMAN

whole thoughts to the cultivation of his respectability.

His good wife, the Lady Lilian Leankettle, who was extravagantly devoted to her husband, shone in the same brilliant manner, and was quoted as a model of gentility by all the good wives of the little community, while Bildith, their charming and handsome daughter, gave every promise of inheriting their interesting ways.

But delightful as all this was to the band of warriors, on Monday morning they were compelled to resume their journey. It was, however, so early when they were ready to start that the gates of the town were not unlocked, so the Honourable Hesketh, with whom, as Mayor of Killgruel, the keys were always left at night, allowed the scout to take the keys and let the wanderers out. After a charmingly polite farewell from the Right Honourable Hesketh and others of their entertainers who had gathered by the town hall to see them off, the gallant band marched down the high street towards the only gate of the town, headed by the intelligent boy scout. From the first the King showed symptoms of being rather unmanageable, and Bill had great difficulty in getting him past the shops, which were now all taking down their shutters, and when they arrived at the sweetstuff shop there was nothing for it but to go in and buy him some cocoanut ice.

At length they managed to get clear of the gates,

THE RESPECTABLE GENTLEMAN

which were then closed with a bang behind them, and the last they saw of the intelligent boy scout was with the great town keys held firmly between his teeth, in order that he might hold with one hand the top of the wall to which he had hastily climbed, while with the other he waved a fond good-bye to the departing wanderers.

With a great gurgling cry, which all took to be one of grief at their departure, the affectionate lad suddenly disappeared and the brave fellows resumed their march.

Their road now took them across the mountains at the foot of which nestled the little town of Killgruel. Towards evening the noble fellows were crossing the highest peaks of the range, weary, and looking forward to their supper and a good night's rest, both of which they proposed to take in the woods on the other side of the mountains. Every one now began to notice that the old King seemed worried about something or other, and the further they marched the more fidgety he became, until at last, when they had nearly descended to the woods on the other side, the old aggravator called his general to him and said:—'Bill, did you happen to notice in the window of the principal sweet-stuff shop in the Killgruel high street, three fine fat sticks of liquorice leaning against the bottle containing the pear drops? Well, I can't get them out of my mind.' Bill tried to persuade him to forget them, and talked of many other things, in order to

THE RESPECTABLE GENTLEMAN

distract him from such thoughts. Presently he appeared to grow easier, and as he did not for some time again refer to the liquorice sticks, Bill was pleased to think that he had been successful in directing the old boy's thoughts into another channel. However, as they were unpacking their things in the woods at which they had now arrived and were lighting fires, preparatory to cooking their suppers, the truly exasperating creature again called Bill to him. 'Bill,' said he, with the most miserable face in the world, 'it's no good. I can't forget 'em, try as I will. I don't want any of that nasty porridge I know they are about to prepare for supper. I must have some of those liquorice sticks.'

Hiding his annoyance as much as he could, Bill tried to convince him how nice porridge really is and how good for him, but the discontented old man, who no doubt had been very much spoilt as a boy, would hear nothing of it. 'I don't want to be done good to,' cried he, 'and if I don't have those liquorice sticks to-night before I go to bed I know I shall get the fidgets and not be able to sleep a wink.'

Bill now pointed out the difficulty of obtaining the liquorice, the distance being so great that it would be impossible to have it brought to the camp before midnight at the very earliest.

The King, however, was obdurate, and Bill was now compelled, much against his will, to summon the whole army together and call for a volunteer

THE RESPECTABLE GENTLEMAN

BOWING POLITELY TO THE PILLAR BOXES

to fetch the liquorice, but not one, not even the pluckful Chad, would venture to return alone to Killgruel along the dreary mountain road in the gathering night. Bill then suggested that two or three should return together and keep each other company, but it was of no avail. At last, the only way out of the difficulty that occurred to Bill was for half the army to return for the liquorice, and the other half to remain in the woods; but here yet another difficulty arose, for no one would stay in the woods with the army weakened to that extent.

At length Bill returned to the whimpering old potentate and once more endeavoured to dissuade

THE CHURCH STEEPLE HAD BEEN REMOVED

him from his selfish purpose, but the more Bill talked, the more obstinate the old King became, and had it not been for the severe training Bill had had as a minder, he must assuredly have lost control of his temper.

'I must have that liquorice,' whined the old grizzler, 'and if there is no other way of obtaining it the whole army must pack up sticks and return to Killgruel.'

Many were the growls of discontent uttered by the poor fellows when Bill gave the necessary orders to pack up again and prepare to return over the mountains. Only by dint of the kindest words did he restrain a mutiny, encouraging them at the same time to humour the old baby and put up with his strange ways until he was restored to his throne, when, no doubt, he would make it up to them in many ways.

THE RESPECTABLE GENTLEMAN

In a little time the brave fellows were all on the march again, but the day was breaking by the time they arrived once more before the walls of Killgruel, all utterly tired, grumpy, and footsore. Bill strode up to the gates of the town, which, of course, at that time of the morning were still closed, and pulled the bell vigorously. He waited some time, and as there was no reply, he pulled the bell again, and then, after another interval, he rang it with all his force, but with no result whatever. He could now, however, hear a great muttering on the other side of the wall and considerable running to and fro, so he determined to wait patiently. At length the little wicket in the gate was opened and one of the Killgruellers looked out, and, recognising Bill and his comrades, hastily shut the wicket again after promising to fetch the Mayor.

Bill now waited a very long time before the wicket opened again, and in the meantime his poor comrades, nearly overcome with their fatigue and their hunger, had set up their camp before the walls and prepared their breakfast, after eating which not one of them was able to keep his eyes open a moment longer, and all fell fast asleep before their fires. Even the old King dozed off and snored peacefully in his tent, forgetting, for the first time in twenty-four hours, the sticks of liquorice, upon the enjoyment of which he had so much set his heart.

THE RESPECTABLE GENTLEMAN

STANDING ALONE UPON THE WALLS

Bill alone of the whole force remained awake, and waited and waited, and as he stood before the gates of the little town, the noise within grew louder and louder until there was a terrific hub-bub within the walls. At last the wicket opened and the face of the respectable Mayor appeared in the little opening, but so altered that at first Bill hardly recognised his good

THE RESPECTABLE GENTLEMAN

host of the day before, so upset and disturbed did he seem.

The poor man then in the most nervous manner explained that no one in the town had seen anything of the boy scout nor of the town keys since he had let the army out of the gate the previous morning, and until they found them it was, of course, impossible to let any one in. However, the good fellow (who certainly seemed rather helpless without his faithful attendant), besought Bill to wait patiently, as they had not yet given up hope of being able to open the gate. The wicket was again hurriedly closed, and Bill, sitting down by the gate, prepared to wait as patiently as he could. So tired, however, was the noble lad, that in spite of all his endeavours to remain awake he soon fell fast asleep. Long and deeply did he slumber, when he was awakened by a most terrible and deafening noise within the town, which had been growing greater and greater during his repose.

Fortunately all in the camp, on account of their great fatigue, were so deep in sleep that the great uproar was unable to awaken them, but Bill at once stood up and scaled the walls to ascertain if possible the cause of the awful din.

The hub-bub was truly deafening, and from his position on the walls Bill could see all over the little town, which was in a shocking state of confusion. The contents of every house were turned into the

THE RESPECTABLE GENTLEMAN

streets, and the distracted inhabitants everywhere hunting amongst the furniture and taking it to pieces in their search for the lost keys. Beds were cut open and discharged their feathers in great clouds that floated about the town; the church steeple had been removed and shaken, and the inside well scoured; many of the good people were descending chimneys attached to lines; pavements were lifted, cellars ransacked, the Town Hall taken to little pieces, old houses pulled down, pillar-boxes cleared out, and lamp-posts blown through by the perplexed and almost frantic Killgruellers in their efforts to find the lost keys. All the milk, the wine, the water, the lemonade and the gravy were being strained through butterfly nets or lawn tennis rackets, and, after melting it down, all the butter, dripping and lard was treated in the same way. The treacle tanks and great reservoirs of linseed tea were thoroughly dragged, but with no result whatever.

A great procession of the townsmen nearly filled the high street which led from the gate to the further end of the town. One by one they approached the gates and tried every key they possessed. All kinds of keys, latch keys, watch keys, cupboard keys, box keys were tried, but not one could be found that would open the lock. To make matters even more unbearable, the respectable Mayor, to whom, of course, every one looked for direction and advice in their trouble, was of no earthly use whatever

THE RESPECTABLE GENTLEMAN

DANGLING BY HIS LEGS

without his scout, upon whom he had so accustomed himself to rely, that he was perfectly helpless without him. His respectability, exert it as much as he would, made no difference of any kind upon the situation, except, perhaps, to place the poor man in everybody's way.

Bill returned to the King who, with the whole camp, was now wide awake, and wondering what on earth was taking place in the town. Bill at once hastened to explain the state of things, in the hope that the old man would at last give up all idea of the

THE RESPECTABLE GENTLEMAN

liquorice; but in this he was much mistaken, for, instead of replying to Bill, the grumpy old provoker turned sulky and would not say a word, so that there was nothing for the poor lad to do but to wait with what patience he could assume.

The day declined, with no lessening of the terrific din within the town, and the gates remained obstinately closed. As evening approached, little clouds of smoke, with now and again a spurt of flame, could be seen rising from the other side of the walls. Presently a single Killgrueller was observed upon the walls, from which he nimbly leapt to the ground on the outer side, and made off round the base of the mountains, in an opposite direction to the camp. Now another appeared and disappeared in the same way; then another and another, and yet another, and then families of two, three, and four. At last whole crowds came scrambling over the walls, and vanished in the same direction, all carrying as many of their belongings as they could conveniently bring along with them.

This went on until all the inhabitants, with the exception of the Mayor, had left the now blazing town, when he was seen standing alone upon the walls. Like the captain of a sinking ship, the noble fellow had waited until all had found safety before he sought it for himself. Bill hastened to assist him in his descent, and no sooner had the poor man reached the ground than Bill led him gently before the King and all the officers of the little army, who were assembled together

The Respectable Gentleman

THE RESPECTABLE GENTLEMAN

watching the flames, and besought him to give them some explanation of these truly unaccountable proceedings of the Killgruellers.

'Alas! and alack-a-day!' sighed the unfortunate gentleman, 'allow me first of all to put four questions to you. Firstly, What is the good of a locked lock without a key?'

They were all forced to admit that it was of no use whatever.

'Secondly, What is the good of a gate with a useless lock that won't unlock?'

No earthly use, all again admitted.

'Thirdly, What is the use of a town if you can't get into it?'

Of course, they all agreed there was only one answer to that.

'And now, fourthly and lastly,' said the Mayor, 'What do you do with all useless things?'

'Destroy them,' Bill promptly rejoined.

'Exactly,' said the Right Honourable Hesketh, 'and that is what we have done with our now useless town, and all the inhabitants are hastening to build another town on the further side of the mountain, the gates of which shall always be nailed open in order that such a dreadful calamity may not occur again.'

Bill somehow could not help thinking that there might have been another way out of the difficulty, but he did not like to say so. The old King at last realised that the Killgruel liquorice was not for him, so he

THE RESPECTABLE GENTLEMAN

offered no serious objections when Bill, early next morning, gave the necessary orders to pack up and prepare for the march, which they now resumed. The respectable gentleman preferred to remain with them rather than again face the unfortunate Killgruellers.

They had not advanced very far upon their road, when Bill, who generally walked a little in advance of his troop, heard a strange clanking noise that appeared to proceed from a tall tree at the wayside. Wondering what odd bird possessed such an unmusical song, he allowed his gaze to wander thoughtfully among the leaves when, suddenly, what should he behold but the form of the vanished scout, dangling by his legs from a branch, and every time the tree was gently stirred by the breeze, there came forth upon the air this weird sound.

Bill hastened to cut him down, but, to his unspeakable surprise, the unhappy young stripling cried, 'Don't, don't! the keys! the keys!' He then explained that when bidding farewell to them the other morning from the walls of Killgruel, in his excitement he had suddenly fallen back and swallowed the keys which, at the time, he had been holding between his teeth. Bill now recalled the strange cry that the poor lad had uttered as they left Killgruel on that occasion. However, in spite of his reluctance to be right side up again until he had recovered the keys, Bill insisted on fetching him down, and, in the severe struggle that ensued, the keys fell out of the boy's throat.

THE RESPECTABLE GENTLEMAN

When at length the army came upon the scene, nothing could exceed the joy of the respectable Mayor at beholding his good attendant, whom he had despaired of ever seeing again. He easily persuaded the willing young creature to remain with him, and share the fortunes of the King of Troy, and thus, with this very welcome addition to their forces, the gallant band marched on.

THE SICILIAN CHAR-WOMAN

THE SICILIAN CHAR-WOMAN

SOME weeks after leaving Killgruel, the noble little band entered a great forest, in the middle of which they overtook a stately char-woman; and no sooner did the Doctor behold her than he left the ranks, and going up to her, shook her kindly by the hand. He then introduced her to the King as the Sicilian Char-woman, and very chatty and pleasant she proved to be, and as she was travelling in the same direction, she graciously entertained them with the story of her life:—

'You may indeed find it more than difficult to

THE SICILIAN CHAR-WOMAN

believe me when I aver that I am the daughter of an Arabian Prince, and that in my early years I was considered not merely the most intelligent, but also the most beautiful and fascinating creature in my father's dominion. As companions in my early childhood I had sixteen elder sisters, all of whom were blessed with singularly affectionate natures, and were generally declared to be only less beautiful and intelligent than myself. No care or expense was spared in our education and in fitting us for the truly exalted position it was hoped that we should occupy, as the daughters of a distinguished Arabian Prince. With this good end in view, the services were secured of the best of music-masters, dancing-masters, and instructors in the many graceful accomplishments that were becoming to our rank; yet, alas! with all that one could reasonably ask for, with every whim and wish gratified almost before it was expressed, with the most indulgent of parents, whose sole joy was to fill our lives with happiness, a settled melancholy by degrees possessed my soul and rendered me unfit to share the youthful pleasures of my sisters. It was not that I was in any way unmindful of all the kindness shown to me in countless ways, but that a craving, always with me since my earliest days, to see the wonderful world I had so often heard described in glowing terms, grew with me as time went by, and, weary of the idle life I led, I longed to use and develop in wider fields the great intelligence I had been gifted with.

THE SICILIAN CHAR-WOMAN

'At first, as was to be expected, my parents would not hear of my leaving them, but seeing that I grew sadder and more discontented day by day, they at length reluctantly gave their consent, for, after all, what greater wish had they than for my happiness.

'After many consultations with the wisest men in my father's court, it was decided that I should take a course of instruction at the Royal Charing College of Sicily, and, on the fateful day, I took leave of my sorrowing parents and sisters, and, in charge of the Grand Vizier, left for Sicily.

'With such good introductions as my father was easily able to command, I had no difficulty in gaining an entry to the College, in which I very soon learnt to distinguish myself. No lack of enthusiasm and industry did I bring to my tasks, and a native ability far above the average soon found opportunities for development, so that in the course of time I was discharged, a fully certified and perfected char-woman.

'Since those early days my skill, my virtues, and my affections have been devoted to the welfare of many families, some of whom were undoubtedly good, some indifferent, while some again were undoubtedly bad. But without any question the worst household of all was that of the Pettigrew Leanmuffins, when first I devoted myself to the wellbeing of its members. Afterwards, however, as you shall hear, their trials,

THE SICILIAN CHAR-WOMAN

together with my disinterested conduct, wrought a reformation in their natures as astounding as it was welcome to all who knew them.

'Mr. Pettigrew Leanmuffins himself, a man of some attainments, though ill-tempered and close to a degree bordering on meanness, had little enough to do with me, hardly ever, indeed, disguising his efforts to ignore my very existence; but no words at my command could describe the ungenerous nature of Mrs. Leanmuffins, who not only refused to concede any little favours to me, such as gracefully offering to entertain my worthy friend the waiter and his respectable family, but even denied, with much asperity, my right to enjoy an afternoon nap on the drawing-room lounge.

'Of no value, in her prejudiced eyes, were the hardly-earned diplomas that had been awarded me during my five years' course at the College, and though richly illuminated with gold, amethysts and pearls, and framed in gorgeously brocaded velvet, she would not hear of my certificates for charing being displayed on the walls of the music-room beside her daughters' certificates for musical proficiency. With such poor examples as their parents constantly before them, it is not to be wondered at that the three daughters, Grillette, Pandalaura, and Blen should discover to one, who would have been their good friend, natures so mean that there seemed little promise of their ever possessing more generous dispositions. Rather, the

THE SICILIAN CHAR-WOMAN

I TOOK LEAVE OF MY SORROWING FATHER

wonder is that they were not really worse than they were, and beyond the chance of any reformation.

'Each valued her own paltry and merely ornamental accomplishments at a far higher rate than my own well proved and certified skill in the serious art of charing, and in their own rude way they never missed an opportunity of reminding me of their fancied superiority.

'During these early years of trial no other consolation had I than the society of the youngest of the Leanmuffin brood—Basil Herbert, one who as yet

THE SICILIAN CHAR-WOMAN

HARDLY DISGUISING HIS EFFORTS TO IGNORE ME

had not developed the mean disposition of his parents and sisters. For hours together, when the other Leanmuffins were away at some jaunt or frolic mayhap, would I, perhaps smarting under some recent indignity, pour forth my troubles into his not unwilling ears. Though but two years of age at the most, he seemed to understand, and I felt that in his own quiet way he gave me his sympathy. I therefore resolved in my young heart that he, at least, should not be spoilt, and to save him from falling to the depths of the other Leanmuffins was now my one hope in life.

THE SICILIAN CHAR-WOMAN

'How often would I, in dumb show, act kind deeds before him in little scenes and plays that I had composed for the purpose, using the kitchen utensils to personify my various characters, thus accustoming his growing mind to kind thoughts, until in time he gave promise of becoming as virtuous as he was handsome.

'He endeared himself to all by his amiable ways, though none suspected to whose loving and untiring care they were due, and friends, nay, even strangers from distant lands travelled to see him, and marvelled at his decorous and kindly behaviour, which charmed as well as astonished all beholders.

'His virtues, however, strong as they were, did not render him immune to the weaknesses to which young children are liable, and in his fifth year he developed a chilblain of the most painful description. Every remedy was tried, dried turnip seed, applications of roasted capers, poultices of wild figs and nard, fomentations of honey and turbot's roe, and many other recipes for the curing of chilblains, recommended by anxious friends. Nevertheless the blain grew chillier and chillier until at last they were compelled to send for a physician.

'The physician, after spending a whole afternoon examining the foot, eventually took the most serious view of the case imaginable, and hastily wrote out the following prescription, promising to call again in a few days:—

Basil Herbert develops a chilblain

THE SICILIAN CHAR-WOMAN

1 Pint New Gruel.
1 gr. Tincture of Green Acorns.
½ gr. Hypo.
1/16 gr. Castor Sugar.
3 Clove Kernels.
½ lb. Coffee Essence.
¾ lb. Sugar of Zinc.
2 gr. Bisulphite of Lead.
1 Pint Spirits of Sulphur.
5 gr. Bicarbonate of Saltpetre.
1 oz. Table Salt.

'Three drops to be mixed in a quart of lukewarm water and gently rubbed into the roots of the blain every five minutes, day and night, until its disappearance, which, if all went well, should take place in about six months' time.

'I was sent out at once, without a "please" or "will you kindly" of course, to the nearest chemist to have the prescription made up. But, alas! he was unable to do it, as he had only three of the necessary ingredients in stock,—the bicarbonate of saltpetre, the table salt, and the hypo. I now went in turn to every chemist in the town, only to find that not one of them could supply me with *all* the necessary ingredients. One perhaps had the tincture of green acorns and the hypo, while another had all but the coffee essence and the clove kernels. Some again only had the spirits of sulphur and the sugar of zinc, and so on. Now, in my despair, I resolved to buy

THE SICILIAN CHAR-WOMAN

each separate ingredient at a different store and mix the prescription myself, but, alas! I was no nearer obtaining it, as no one could supply me with the clove kernels. Determined to succeed, I visited in succession every town in Sicily, but not a single clove kernel could I find from one end of the island to the other.

'As I stood on the sea-shore at the edge of the island wondering what next I should do to complete the prescription, my thoughts flew across the sea to my home in Arabia, and I decided to return there at once in the hope of learning from my parents where I should be most likely to find the kernels.

'With the other ingredients securely sewn into the lining of my skirt, I embarked for Arabia, and in due course arrived at my father's palace.

'When my good parents recognised me, which they did only after some minutes of close scrutiny, for it was at least twenty-five years since I had left home, they extended to me the kindliest welcome, and by their affectionate conduct dispelled any restraint I might have felt after so long an absence. In the meanwhile each of my sixteen sisters had married a Sultan or Prince at the very least, and they were now reigning in truly regal splendour in different parts of the world, and my parents, being alone in their old age, begged of me to come and live with them and gladden their declining years. This, however, I soon convinced them I could not do, and besought their help

THE SICILIAN CHAR-WOMAN

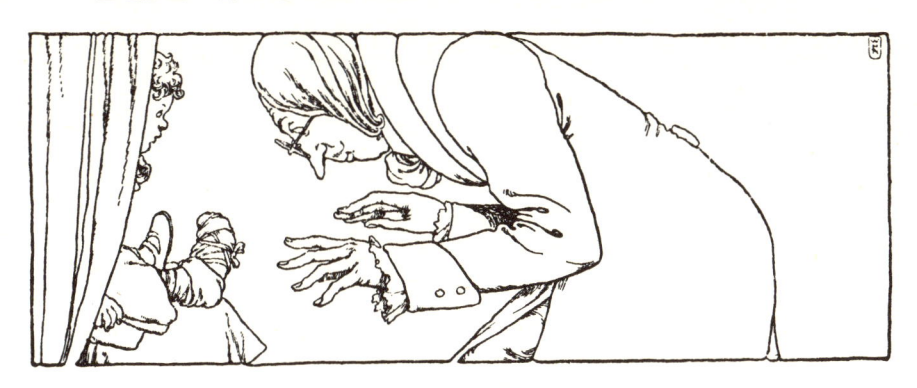

THEY WERE COMPELLED TO SEND FOR A PHYSICIAN

and advice in my quest. The Prince, my father, manifested the greatest desire to assist me, and took a fatherly interest in my fortunes. He caused the palace to be ransacked from top to bottom, but with no success,—there was not a single clove kernel to be found in the place.

'After an affectionate parting with my father and mother, I visited every one of my married sisters in turn, each of whom introduced me to her husband and friends with considerable pride, for you must know that already my fame as a char-woman of great ability had reached even to the most distant parts. One and all were equally felicitous in their expressions of delight at seeing me, and equally pressing in their invitations to me to take up my abode with them. Yet none were able to help me in the quest I had so much at heart.

'At last I returned to Sicily without the clove kernels, and, too ashamed to appear before the Lean-

THE SICILIAN CHAR-WOMAN

muffins without the completed prescription, I wandered about the island in despair, resting at night in the caves of the mountains, satisfying the cravings of my hunger on the hard dry leaves of the cactus.

'I now bethought me of my good friend the waiter and the willingness he had consistently evinced to help me when in trouble, and once more I embarked, this time for the shores of Lombardy, at which place I knew he had a comfortable situation. With very little difficulty I found the refreshment establishment at which he worked, and, as I anticipated, he was extremely pleased to meet me again, and manifested the liveliest joy at the prospect of being of some help to me. Together we studied the menu of the day very thoroughly, but could find no mention whatever of clove kernels, and then, idly looking through some menus of recent date, handsomely bound together for future reference, we discovered that clove kernels had been served as recently as the day before. It would be useless to attempt to describe the despair that took possession of me when I discovered that I had only missed them by one day. The waiter excitedly rushed down to the kitchen to see if any had been left over, but, alas! there was not a single clove kernel to be found in the larder or anywhere else. On leaving the refreshment rooms I shed the bitterest tears that had ever fallen from my usually joyful eyes, and on the rocks by the sea gave way to a mood of the greatest despondency.

THE SICILIAN CHAR-WOMAN

'More ashamed than ever to return to the Leanmuffins, I made several inquiries for any one requiring the services of an amicable, virtuous, and, at the same time, experienced char-woman, determined to find work in Lombardy if any were to be had.

'Not receiving satisfactory replies to my inquiries, my good waiter, true to his kind nature, introduced me to one of his most regular customers, the Marquis of Lombardy, who had been looking out for some years for a capable char-woman to superintend the management of his domestic affairs. Meeting with the approval of the Marquis, I thus secured a comfortable home, and resolved to forget that I had ever lived in Sicily.

'Now it happened that the Marquis, being a regular diner at the restaurant, had partaken of clove kernels on the last occasion they were served, and three or four must have fallen from his spoon into his waistcoat pocket at the time, for I overheard his valet repeat to the housemaid that he had found them therein when brushing his master's clothes, and that he had presented them to one of the boatmen's children. Learning the name of the child, not a moment did I lose in hunting for him high and low, and eventually discovered him playing idly on the sands with what, I was convinced, were the kernels I so much coveted. At last, thought I, they are within my reach, and running joyfully up to the light-

THE SICILIAN CHAR-WOMAN

hearted lad discovered, alas! that he was only playing with brass buttons.

'After the first shock of my new disappointment had passed away, I questioned the lad as to how he had disposed of the clove kernels, and he told me that his father, who considered them excellent bait, had taken them from him and given him three brass buttons in exchange.

'On asking him where his father was at the present moment, he pointed with his sunburnt hand to the horizon, and looking in the direction indicated, I perceived a little fishing-smack, miles away. Without the loss of a single second, I hired a boat, and, with a boatman to assist, rowed in pursuit, and after a chase of three or four hours drew up, in an exhausted condition, alongside the smack. I now in piteous tones begged the clove kernels of the weather-beaten mariner, but he only laughed loudly and bitterly in reply, and, on my inquiring the reason of his cruel mirth, told me in faltering accents that he had only just hauled in his lines to discover that the fish had gone off with the bait and hook as well. Thus doomed to disappointment, I spent the rest of the day in a state of mind bordering on madness.

'It was a little time after this that, one evening, I was sitting over the kitchen fire. The cook had just served up an excellent dish of fish, and my mind was still turning to Sicily in spite of my endeavours to forget that there was such a place, and wondering if

THE SICILIAN CHAR-WOMAN

THE IMPROVEMENT WAS MAINTAINED

ever I should see Basil Herbert again. Suddenly there was a most terrible disturbance overhead in the dining-room, a noise as of plates being thrown from one end of the room to the other, and presently wild shrieks and groans of pain. I ran lightly upstairs, always ready to be of use in emergencies of any kind, and opened the dining-room door just in time to see the Marquis raving most pitifully. It transpired that the very identical fish that had swallowed the hook

THE SICILIAN CHAR-WOMAN

DISCOVERED A CLOVE KERNEL

and the clove kernels had been caught and served up to the Marquis's table, and he, poor man, had just swallowed the hook. Taking in the situation at a glance, I soon saw the probability that the three clove kernels, or one or two of them, were in the body of the fish, and walking boldly into the room I grasped the fish by the tail, and took to my heels.

'For miles I ran, out of the town and into the country without stopping, until, quite exhausted and out of breath, I sat down beneath a rock to rest. I now examined the fish which I still held in my hand, and found only two of the kernels in its body, the Marquis having probably swallowed the third.

'However, although not the complete number required by the prescription, they were better than no clove kernels at all, so after resting awhile I resolved to return once more to Sicily.

'After some vicissitudes I arrived at last at the

THE SICILIAN CHAR-WOMAN

home of the Leanmuffins to find them all in despair. Basil Herbert's condition had not improved, and the physician had ceased his visits and gone in search of me. I soon mixed the stuff, which brought some little relief to the unhappy young patient—but not enough, as the lotion was not sufficiently strong without the third clove kernel.

'We persevered, however, and the improvement was just maintained. At last one evening when all the members of the family were gathered round the sufferer's bed endeavouring to distract him by every manner of entertainment conceivable and by cheerful songs, glees, and the telling of interesting stories, there came a low knock at the door and somebody inquiring for me. Who should it be but my faithful friend the waiter, who, on sweeping the floor of the Lombardic refreshment room, had discovered a little clove kernel in the corner, and, mad with delight at being able to assist me, had hastened from Lombardy to bring me the treasure. Small though it was, it was enough to give the requisite strength to the lotion, and in due course the young patient completely recovered.

'After their severe trials the Leanmuffins were completely transformed; from being ignoble, mean, and unkind, they became generous in the extreme. Their joy knew no bounds, and henceforth they made me quite one of their family, and my friend the waiter and his good people were asked to dine with us every Sunday that they were in Sicily.

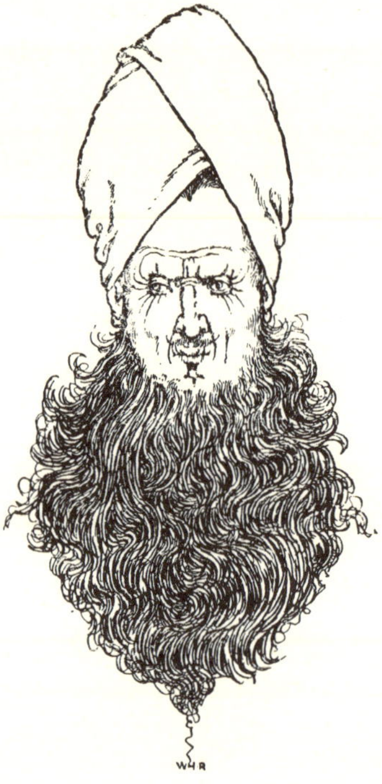
WHR

THE INTERVAL

'THE INTERVAL'

WHEN the Sicilian Char-woman had finished the narration of her truly wonderful experiences, and while the army were yet applauding her, the King stepped down from his chair, and taking the good woman by the hand, explained to her the object of their great expedition. 'And now,' said the astute old monarch in conclusion, 'powerful

'THE INTERVAL'

as we undoubtedly are, and as you can see for yourself that we are, we have yet one weakness, and that weakness is, that we cannot boast of a single char-woman of any description within our ranks. It has occurred to us, in listening to your story, that if you are able, as I have no doubt you will be, to obtain a good character from your last place, that we shall be delighted to engage you as an assistant to the amiable Boadicea in her attendance upon my person.'

'Fiddlesticks,' snapped the abrupt woman, 'look after your person indeed! Look after it yourself,' and the strange creature walked off. Unwilling to lose such a treasure, the King called after her, and explained that if he had offended her it was quite unintentionally, and offered her any post she would like to fill, of course providing that it had not already been filled, in his army.

'Now you are talking reasonably,' replied the quickly mollified creature. 'Well, as you are so very kind, I don't mind being the flag-bearer.'

'But I am really afraid we have no flag,' objected the King.

'Oh, we'll soon settle that little difficulty,' replied the woman. And she at once removed her apron and snatching from the astonished Scout the staff he usually carried with him, she tied the apron thereto by its two strings and waved it proudly in the air three or four times, at each time jumping as high as she could.

'THE INTERVAL'

Every one cheered in their delight at the readiness of the good woman, and congratulated each other cordially on this interesting addition to their forces.

The King now stood up in his chair, and after quieting the general excitement by ringing his bell, he thus addressed his troops:—

'My dear old boys and girls, although, no doubt, I appear to you a very fine man indeed, with a good appetite and fairly well covered for my time of life, I am not quite the man I should be. You must know that in my early babyhood I was a victim to the wicked carelessness of the royal cook. One morning this thoughtless creature left an unboiled parsnip on the garden path (had it been boiled and soft, my fate had been different perhaps) while chatting with a friend at the tradesmen's entrance. As ill luck would have it, I was at the time playing on the palace roof, to which I had climbed through the nursery chimney, and, childlike, was gazing curiously at a strange bird flying overhead, when I overbalanced and fell from the roof right on to the parsnip on the garden path, which, as you will guess, hurt me very severely indeed.'

The King here exhibited to his audience a dent on his head in the form of a parsnip.

'On hearing of this my father, of course, was highly indignant, and ordered the cook to be beheaded instantly, or, at all events, as soon as she had finished cooking the dinner.

'The dinner, however, was so excellent that my

'THE INTERVAL'

I FELL ON TO THE PARSNIP

father, in his enjoyment of it, forgot all about my mishap, and the cook went unpunished. Nevertheless the shock to my system was so great that, feeling it even to this day, as I have said, I am not the man I should be. A trifle irritable now and again; or more sulky and disagreeable than I care to admit; or at times even harsh, morose, surly, snappish, rattish, and short-tempered, all little failings you have no doubt noticed, and which now, knowing my early misfortune, you will more readily excuse.

'Well,' continued the King, 'you will at least understand that a little rest is good for me now and again, so that, as we have already travelled half the distance to my kingdom, I intend to give you all a whole holiday to-morrow, and on the day following, which happens to be my birthday, I will celebrate the great occasion with a grand review, after which we shall once more resume our long journey.'

'THE INTERVAL'

THEY ALL ONCE MORE STARTED

This welcome announcement was received with the greatest enthusiasm by the brave fellows, and loud cheers echoed again and again through the forest, and a great feast was at once prepared.

Seated in a circle on the grass beneath the trees, the good souls enjoyed to the full the simple fare before them, and then, after once more cheering the old monarch, retired to their tents to sleep, and to dream of the morrow in store for them.

Next morning, with the exception of the old King,

'THE INTERVAL'

ON THEIR ADVENTUROUS JOURNEY

who intended to rest and remain in bed all day, every one was up betimes. After a hearty meal, Bill explained to them all the dangers of the great forest, and the necessity of returning to camp at dusk. Then, taking care not to disturb the King, they all left the camp, different parties taking different directions, seeking amusement wherever they could find it.

Bill took care of his charges, who had the greatest sport in the world,—tree-climbing, nutting, chasing butterflies, fishing in the pools, playing at Wild Indians, Hunt-the-Stag, Robbers and Thieves, Poor Jenny is a-weeping, Red Rover, and every really sensible game that there is to play, while Boadicea spent the time very happily in making beautiful bunches of wild flowers.

Chad, however, was a bit of a nuisance, crying all the morning because he was not allowed to eat toadstools; so to keep him out of mischief, Bill tied him to the highest branch of a very tall tree, and there left him to have his cry out.

The Long Man took Ptolemy Jenkinson in hand, and taught him how to bird-nest, at the same time adding to his own valuable collection of eggs. The Ancient Mariner made a swing for the Absent-minded Indian, and wondered, while he was swinging him to and fro, whether he enjoyed it or not, for the thoughtful creature's face still gave no sign at all of what was taking place in his mind, supposing he had one. The Doctor spent the day upside down, with his feet supported against the trunk of a tree and his nose on the ground, while he studied the habits of the stag-beetle. The Boy Scout practised scouting by continually losing his patron and then finding him again, while the Respectable Gentleman himself kept his respectability in hand by behaving most politely to all the trees of the forest,—raising his hat to the silver-birches, leaving his card on the ash-trees, introducing a hornbeam to a blackthorn, apologising to

And left him to have his cry out

'THE INTERVAL'

the thistles for treading on their lower leaves, and, in fact, behaving like the perfect gentleman he was, and having a really enjoyable day.

The Triplets played hide-and-seek, and the Sicilian Char-woman set to and dusted and scrubbed down a good number of the forest trees, and spent the rest of the day in endeavouring to clear up the last year's leaves that everywhere littered the grass.

It was quite late in the evening when all returned to camp, quite tired out, and after supper each crept quietly to bed without awakening the King, and soon the whole camp was fast asleep.

In the morning every one awoke in the best of spirits, and brimful of the many things they had to tell of the happy time they had spent the day before. The old monarch seemed much refreshed for his long rest, and before sitting down to breakfast every one in turn went up to him and shook the happy old boy by the hand, wishing him many happy returns, after which they all sat down and enjoyed a substantial breakfast. Before the repast was quite finished, and while the King was looking the other way, Bill walked round the ring formed by the army as they sat upon the grass, and collected birthday presents for the old monarch. Every one was delighted to give something to His Majesty to show how much they appreciated his greatness, and when the old chap received the many gifts, all done up in one brown paper parcel, he was so overcome that he could hardly stammer forth

'THE INTERVAL'

THE WHOLE CAMP WAS FAST ASLEEP

his thanks. And this is what he found in the parcel when, with trembling hands, he had succeeded in opening it :—

From Bill,	. . . .	A bone-handled, two-bladed pocket-knife, a little rusted, but with only one blade missing.
From Noah,	. . . .	Some string.
From Ratchett,	. . .	8 brace buttons (very bright).
From the Twins { Quentin,	.	Wooden top of peg-top.
{ Hannibal,	.	Iron peg of same.
From Randall,	. . .	Ferrule of umbrella.
From Nero,	. . . .	More string.

'THE INTERVAL'

From Biddulph, . . .	Dial of old watch (not cracked very much).
From Knut, ...	Glass marble (beautifully coloured).
From Chad, ...	2 pear drops (old, but in good condition).
From the other children collectively, . . .	Twenty last year's horse chestnuts on string (very hard).
From the Ancient Mariner, .	Piece of wood skilfully cut into the form of a pebble.
From the Absent-Minded Indian, ...	Nothing.
From the Triplets, . .	3 bunches of violets.
From the Respectable Gentleman, ...	His visiting-card.
From the Boy Scout, . .	One of the Killgruel town-keys he had swallowed.
From the Sicilian Char-woman,	Small piece of soap.
From the Long Man, . .	Wren's egg.
From Boadicea, . . .	A hat full of ripe blackberries.
From the Doctor, . . .	Half of cough lozenge.
From Ptolemy Jenkinson, .	A last year's ticket for a box.

Every one clamoured for a speech, but the old fellow was so affected by all this unexpected kindness, that he would not trust himself to open his mouth, so with tears of gratitude pouring from his eyes, he retired to his chair. These interesting proceedings thus coming to an end, he was wheeled into the forest by Boadicea until they came to the open space where the review was to take place.

'THE INTERVAL'

Having dried his eyes and smartened himself up, with Boadicea standing sedately at his side holding the presents, the King now solemnly awaited the appearance of the troops. Soon there was a great noise in the direction of the camp, and then they could be heard approaching.

First came the nine brave sons of Crispin and Chloe, proudly marching three by three, and as they passed the King each gallantly saluted him. Now followed the stately Char-woman with the flag held aloft, and when she came opposite His Majesty she jumped magnificently three times into the air. She was followed by more of Bill's charges, and then, with great dignity, Bill, the King's general, marched past the Royal Old Boy and saluted him grandly.

Another detachment of Bill's charges followed the general, then the Ancient Mariner approached, and, after placing the Absent-minded Indian on the ground, he, with much dignity, saluted the King by touching his forelock, sailor fashion, and after a few steps of the hornpipe, once more resumed his burden and moved on. The Ancient Mariner was followed by the Long Man who winked knowingly at the King as he passed by. Ptolemy Jenkinson came next, then the Doctor, who, not knowing quite what was expected of him, proceeded to feel the King's pulse, but was quickly hustled off by the Scout, who now approached.

The Respectable Gentleman followed the Boy Scout, and raised his hat in a very gentlemanly

'THE INTERVAL'

manner to the King as he passed him and politely handed him one of his cards, upon which he had scribbled a few good wishes to the old monarch.

Now, one by one, the Triplets passed in front of the delighted King, before whom each of the sweet creatures performed the most graceful curtsy, and the procession then terminated with another detachment of Bill's charges.

The King was more than satisfied, and they all once more started on their adventurous journey.

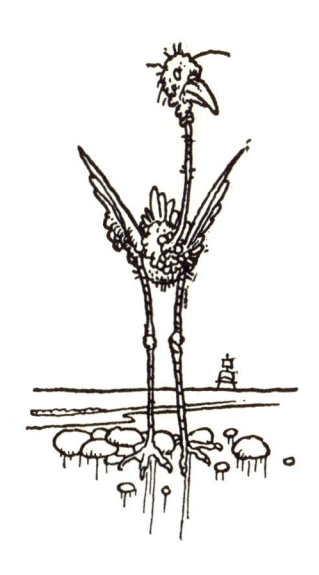

THE REAL SOLDIER

THE REAL SOLDIER

AFTER travelling some days, they came across a real soldier seated at the side of the road, and Bill at once persuaded the King to invite so valuable a man to join their expedition. The King therefore left his chariot and approached him, and asked the noble-looking fellow if he would care to make one of their party, and, if so, whether he had a good character from his last general, and the old warrior replied:—

THE REAL SOLDIER

'Allow me, my good sirs, to recite to you one of my most noteworthy achievements, one of which, peradventure, you may not have read in the numerous books filled with accounts of my exploits. I shall thus remove any trace of doubt that may linger in your minds as to my great courage and astute generalship.

All expressing their eagerness to hear the story, the wordful old warrior proceeded:—

'As near as I can remember, it was in the early fifties when, a mere drummer-boy, with the bloom of early boyhood still gracing my brave young cheek, I marched with the gallant 53rd or, as you may possibly know them, the King's Own Royal Roebucks, to the relief of the Isle of Wight. This island, at the time I mention, was blockaded by that notorious filibuster, Reginald Bendbrisket, a rogue who, possessed of the greatest audacity and cunning, had earned for himself an unenviable reputation, from Margate to Samoa, by the terrible extent of his depredations.

'You will all doubtless remember how, disappointed in his endeavours to usurp the throne of Pitcairn Island, he had impudently resolved to make a sudden raid upon the Isle of Wight; and thus to feed his own insatiable greed and, at the same time, appease the disappointed rage of his desperate followers, he would have plunged the peaceful little island into abject misery. What tempted him thereto none

THE REAL SOLDIER

can guess with any certainty, unless indeed it were the many false reports, spread abroad by the unscrupulous, of the gold, silver, and diamonds to be found there; of the extensive quarries, rich in the finest hearthstone; and of the natural paraffin springs, that could provide the world with the purest oil; and many other reports, alike false and discreditable to their inventor and to those who repeated them to the credulous stranger.

'Had the rogue been successful in his latest raid, his small band of followers (mayhap increased to a powerful army by the hordes of discontented periwinkle-gatherers, prawners, and lobster-potterers that earn a scanty living on our shores) would, without doubt, have had at their mercy the Isle of Sheppey and the numerous other Islets that ornament our coasts. And then, from these a sudden and successful descent on Ludgate Hill would have rendered him master of the whole of London. Now I am going to tell you how the courage and forethought of a simple drummer-boy frustrated all his schemes, and brought to his knees one of the most unscrupulous enemies that has ever invaded our shores.

'To come back to the beginning of my story, we had a comfortable journey down, the tedium of which had been greatly relieved by delightful conversation and intellectual chatting, each in his turn considerably astounding the others by the amount of intelligence he displayed. These pursuits were again

THE REAL SOLDIER

varied by interesting recitations, and such parlour-games as could be conveniently played in a railway carriage. We arrived in the afternoon at a snug little hamlet on the coast opposite the island, whence we embarked in a fleet of disused barges and dredgers. We reached our destination, after a fairly calm voyage, without having excited the curiosity of the invaders, only one of whose vessels we passed, and all on board it were so engrossed with the captain, who was violently sea-sick, that we passed unobserved.

'We were 2,352 strong, including the gallant 53rd, of which I was a member, a battery of artillery, a camel corps, two squadrons of the smartest cavalry that ever chased a rabbit across the Hackney Marshes, and a battalion of infantry, so well trained that there was not one of the rank and file who could not play quite delightfully on the piano; while the officers were unexcelled at conjuring tricks, with which they used to amuse the soldiers seated round the camp-fires of an evening. We were ably generalled by that best of all officers, Sir Francis Melville Glowmutton, whose fame in after years very nearly earned for him the honour of being mentioned in a popular Encyclopædia.

'We were met on the beach by a procession of the inhabitants, headed by the president of the island, all of whom were delighted to see us, and extended to us the most hospitable of welcomes. Without waiting

THE REAL SOLDIER

for formal introductions, they fraternised in the most friendly spirit with the troops who, in turn, were charmed with their reception and, being quite beyond themselves with gratification, adorned their conversation with the most graceful compliments to the inhabitants and grateful tributes to their kindness.

'The blockade had lasted barely eight weeks, so that, as yet, the inhabitants of the island were not aware of it, and when they learnt from the soldiers the real state of affairs, they rejoiced beyond measure, and redoubled their congratulations to the army and to each other, and the president seized the very first opportunity publicly to thank the general for his thoughtfulness in coming to relieve them.

'For quite a long time the handshaking went on, and every one was so amiably excited that the president, anxious that so much good feeling should not be thrown away, invited every one to spend the evening with him at his presidency on the Needles.

'And such a bright and happy evening it was too! Every one in the best of spirits, and entering blithely into all the games! "Oranges and Lemons," "Nuts and May," and "Poor Jenny is a-weeping," had never, within the memory of any one present, been played with greater zest, and, what was more wonderful, never had the rather trying game of "Hunt the Slipper" provoked less ill-temper since it was first introduced into this country at the Norman Conquest.

THE REAL SOLDIER

THE REAL SOLDIER

'The joy of the frolicsome ones was only equalled by that of the older inhabitants and the elderly officers, who, seated on chairs placed for them round the walls of the hall, fairly shook with laughter and merriment, until the tears rolled down their handsome old cheeks.

'At last, with flushed and happy faces, all sat down to a splendid cold supper provided by the President, but it was some little time before the feast could proceed, as every one was so well-behaved that there was quite a turmoil of passing things to one another. At last, however, every one was served, and the supper proceeded with the greatest mirth on all sides.

'After a while the president stood up to make a speech, and had only got as far as, "Ladies and Gentlemen, it is not that we——" when, to everybody's consternation, there was a loud knock at the door and, without waiting to be asked, in stalked the notorious Reginald himself.

'Having approached the table, he slowly withdrew his gaze from the refreshments (to which it had wandered on his entry), and, drawing himself to his greatest height, demanded of the president the instant surrender of the island to him as his rightful property, averring that it had been left to him by an aunt, whose favourite he had been. Then, putting his hand to his bosom, he drew thence an old roll of parchment which, indeed, proved to be the Will of one Martha Grub. This he handed to the president, who read aloud

THE REAL SOLDIER

therefrom the following clause, which had been underlined :—

'And I do bequeath unto my good sister's son, the shapely Reginald Bendbrisket, inasmuch as he has shown some kindness unto my black cat, now dead alas! twenty jars of the good plum preserve I did make last fall as well as five yards of the good garden hose wherewith I did heretowhile water my cabbages in the droughty seasons, the rest to be cut up and divided equally amongst my other nephews and nieces to be used by them as they may see fit whatsoever.

'At their demise the said pieces shall be delivered up to the said Reginald, who will once more unite the fragments and pass the completed hose on to his heirs for ever.

'For his goodness in undertaking thus to carry out my wishes I do also bequeath unto the beforementioned Reginald the Island of Wight situate at the south coast of England.

'On reading this the president turned very pale and every one trembled, never having dreamt of the strength of the invader's position. But being a bit of a lawyer, the president very soon rallied and replied to the filibuster, in as courtly a manner as he could assume, that he was bound to admit that his aunt Martha had, without doubt, left the island to him, and that he would be the last man to dispute the fact—here the rogue, vainly imagining that he was about to realise his greatest hopes, could not conceal his satisfaction,

THE REAL SOLDIER

'BUT HOLD!' CRIED THE PRESIDENT

and helped himself to a sandwich—"But hold!" cried the president in a terrible voice, "I do dispute that it was hers to leave."

'At this the irascible Reginald completely lost his temper and hurled the sandwich with such fury to the ground that it broke one of the gorgeous tiles that ornamented the floor. "Have you," said he, "the audacity to doubt the word of my aunt Martha? Have you the face to stand there and dispute the will of that excellent woman, written when dying of a broken heart at the death of her black cat, and whose only solace was the company of her dutiful nephew? Then

Reginald completely lost his temper

THE REAL SOLDIER

'YOUR FATE BE UPON YOUR OWN HEAD'

your fate be upon your own head." And he strode out of the hall gnashing and grinding his teeth in the most terrible manner, only stopping to pick up the sandwich which he had thrown down in his outburst of passion.

'When the door had slammed to with terrific force behind him there was a great silence in the hall, and we all looked at one another with scared faces. Soon every one arose from the table, and silently left the banqueting-hall to prepare for the fight which we now knew would come on the morrow.

'Try as I would, I could not sleep for thinking of

the battle in store for us. I counted more sheep than would have fed our army for six months, but with no result. I then tried elephants, and after that camels and zebras, and finally, hoping that their odd shapes might bring me repose, I tried ant bears, but all in vain. At last, in despair, I rose from my hard couch, donned my uniform, and snatching up a cracknel, strode out of my tent.

'Murmuring "Brittle Pantechnicons" (which, by the way, was our password) to the sentry, I strolled idly down to the sea. It was a beautiful and perfectly still night, with not a ripple to disturb the surface of the sea, upon which, here and there, would glow a little shimmer of light as the phosphorescent turbot rose to its prey. In the distance, and away to the right, could be seen the camp-fires of the enemy, and the reflections in the pools left by the tide. Ever and anon sounds of merriment could be heard as the invaders, heedless of the morrow, spent the night in revelry. To the left, and further back, could be seen the tents of our forces, not a sound arising therefrom except the low monotonous breathing of the soldiers (who were so well drilled that even in their sleep they breathed in time), or maybe the "Who goes there?" of the sentry would sound in the darkness, as he mistook a moth for a spy, or the drone of the beach bee for the war-whoop of the enemy.

'At the water's edge, dark against the starry sky, I found a solitary bathing-machine, beneath which

THE REAL SOLDIER

FLOUNDERING ABOUT IN THE SEA

I crept, and here at length my weariness quite overcame me and I slept. How long I remained thus I cannot tell, but I was awakened by heavy footsteps on the floor of the machine over my head. My curiosity was intense, but resisting the temptation to rush out and satisfy it, I wisely resolved to remain in my present position as long as possible.

'Presently the mysterious tenant of the machine opened its seaward door and stood revealed in the light of the moon, which had arisen during my sleep, as the terrible Reginald Bendbrisket himself, clothed in a deep black bathing-suit. I crouched down, not daring to move a muscle, and was presently relieved to see him, after standing for some time on the steps of the machine, amble carefully over the stones to the edge of the sea, into which he plunged.

'Now it was that an idea suddenly occurred to me, and I instantly crept from my place of concealment, and stealing up to the landward door of the machine nailed it fast with the hammer and nails I always carried with me to mend my drum, which was not infrequently broken beneath my enthusiastic blows.

THE REAL SOLDIER

Having secured the front door, I now crept in at the back and, doffing my own clothes, soon donned those of the unconscious filibuster, who was still floundering about in the sea. Having effected this change, I crept back to my former position under the machine, and had barely made myself comfortable there when I saw the rogue returning.

'After scrambling painfully over the stony beach he mounted the steps and entered the machine, and the slam of the door as it closed upon him was the signal for me to rush out and secure this as I had already secured the front door. Having done this, I waited no longer, but made off with all possible speed in the direction of the enemy's camp, which I had nearly reached, when I heard a most terrible banging from the interior of the now distant bathing-machine. Losing no time, I entered the camp, and, being easily mistaken for their captain, passed on unchallenged.

'Arriving in time at the centre of the camp, I found all the men gathered together, having forsaken their revels, evidently in expectation of the return of their leader.

'Standing before the villainous crew, I assumed, as nearly as I could, the mien and rough harsh voice of their filibustering captain, and ordered them to embark at once and to leave the island, as it had been reinforced during the night by such a mass of thundering artillery as would be impossible to withstand, and

THE REAL SOLDIER

IN EXPECTATION OF THEIR LEADER

that they were even now fast approaching along the beach from the other end of the island where they had landed. The men, on hearing this appeared quite incredulous and their growls of disbelief grew louder and louder and threatened a terrible mutiny. Having at length gained a hearing, I invited them all to that part of the camp by which I had entered, to hear for themselves the approach of the distant hosts. Leading them all, still grumbling and growling, a little way beyond the camp, I commanded them all to be absolutely quiet, and then, in the silence which ensued, could be heard far away in the direction of

THE REAL SOLDIER

the bathing-machine a most terrific and continuous banging, together with the sound of muffled shouting.

'The men were aghast, and in the moonlight their swarthy faces could be seen to change to a ghastly white. Then, with an unearthly yell, they all turned and fled in a wild panic to the boats. They tumbled over and over each other in their anxiety to get away, and many got wet to the skin in their endeavour to reach the boats. At last, to my great joy, I saw the last of them pull off and reach the ships, which now put on all sail and vanished away for ever.

'I now returned to the bathing-machine, from which still came a terrible din, though not quite so violent as it had been at first.

'Taking hold of the rope that was fastened to it, I began to drag the machine in the direction of our camp, the banging meanwhile gradually subsiding, until at last only an occasional bang proclaimed the machine to be inhabited. As before, I passed the sentry by murmuring "Brittle Pantechnicons" and drew the machine up in front of the General's tent.

'The General, having finished an early breakfast, was just setting out to take a stroll before settling down to plan out the battle, and seeing me, whom he at first took to be Reginald Bendbrisket, the good man received quite a severe shock. However, I soon undeceived him, and after relating my adventures I unfastened the door of the bathing-machine, and

THE REAL SOLDIER

disclosed therein the form of the filibuster on bended knees, imploring our mercy.

'Every one was delighted at such a speedy end to the campaign, for my part in which I was duly honoured. Reginald Bendbrisket, after a mild punishment, reformed and became a very respectable gentleman, the president kindly using his influence to secure for him a lucrative position in a well-known Insurance Office.

'And thus, my good Sirs, it is, that the Isle of Wight still remains one of our many valued possessions.'

'The very man for me,' thought the King of Troy, when he had finished his story, and before proceeding with their journey, he promoted the martial creature to the high position of second General-in-chief of the army.

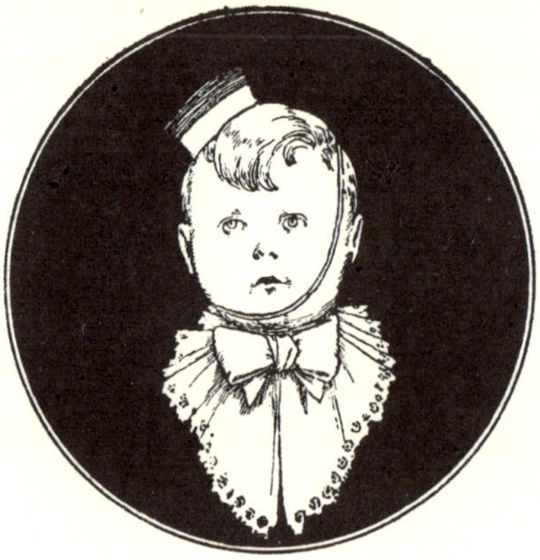

THE WILD MAN

THE WILD MAN

ONE day the army were overtaken by a singularly wild-looking man who proved, however, to be at the same time quite an amiable creature, and expressed a great desire to seek some employment with the gallant fellows. The King was pleased to enlist the nice and sociable person, and was more than repaid for his confidence in him by his charming ways. On one occasion, when the King was rather tired and worried, the Wild Man, in order to distract the dear old fellow, told the following story :—

THE WILD MAN

'Good Sirs, though wild enough indeed, yet may I claim to be an unspoilt child of nature, whose finest instincts have, unchecked, found their true development. Thus, communing with nature from my cradle and living on terms of the closest intimacy with her wildest creatures, I can appreciate their humble wants, their hopes and fears, and have acquired the truly marvellous power of conversing with these simple-minded denizens of the wilderness.

'My home was a rocky cave hard by the sea-shore, in which I lived in simple happiness with my good wife, now dead, alas! this many a long year ago, and our five brown children, who long since have grown to men and gone out into the world to seek their fortunes. Harmless indeed were our joys, and our trials we bore with that great fortitude which was not the least of the blessings we derived from our simple mode of life.

'To proceed with my tale, on one dismal evening late in autumn, I left my cave, with the hungry cries of my children still in my ears,—for, indeed, the poor things had had no sup or bite the whole day through. Wondering what I could do that they might not go supperless to bed, I strolled along the sands by the sea in the hope of finding some odd limpet or whelk which, together with a few dried dandelion leaves, might make a simple stew. Alas! no vestige of a single crustacean could I find, so I sat me down upon the sands, determined not to return until the children

THE WILD MAN

had fallen asleep on the dry ferns and grass heaped up for them at the back of the cave, as their cries were more torment to me than my own emptiness.

'The sun had long ago set, and the autumnal twilight, reflected in the pools of still water left by the far receded tide, was gradually fading from the sky, when I fancied I could hear a low heart-rending moan from off the desolate waste of sand before me. Again and again it sounded, and at last realising that it might be uttered by some creature in distress, I stood up and, as far as the fading light would permit, scanned the sands in every direction.

'Nothing, however, could I see, and as the moan still continued at intervals and became, in fact, more and more painful and beseeching, I wandered about, a prey to the liveliest anxiety, endeavouring to discover whence it proceeded.

'At length I perceived on the sand, at a little distance before me, a small dark motionless object, and at that instant a harrowing sound, arising therefrom on the evening air, left me in no doubt as to the origin of the moans I had already heard. Creeping as quietly as possible on my hands and knees quite close to it, I found it to be a lovely blue point oyster, and bringing my head to a level with the shell, I asked coaxingly, and in as soft a voice as I could command, what ailed it.

'"Alas!" said the oyster, "a little while ago I possessed a child as sweet as ever chortled to its

Harmless indeed were our joys

THE WILD MAN

I PLEADED MY CASE

gasping mother, but snatched from me as it has been by the cruellest of whelks, it may even now lie helpless in the grasp of the ravenous brute, as it ruthlessly sups off its delicate limbs. No such grief have I had since that old native, my worthy husband, was slain, and was laid in state, his hoary head supported by a slice of lemon, beside a piece of brown bread-and-butter."

'Deeply affected by her grief, I begged her to reveal the name of the little one and to indicate the direction taken by the marauding whelk. "Bertram is its name," said the widowed blue point, and I could

THE WILD MAN

hear the tears falling within the shell as, with her beard, she pointed out the path followed by the rogue.

'I had not proceeded far in the direction indicated when I overtook a whelk, whose face was quite distorted by a savage look, and whose growls drowned the feeble cries of a tender blue pointlet whom he dragged along by the beard.

'"Now what is all this about?" said I to the sullen fellow. "Why should you, who are maybe blessed with young of your own, rob a poor widowed oyster of her only consolation since the death of her husband? A heart of rock would have melted at the cries of your victim, but you, ungenerous, can have no heart at all, and entirely drag the name of whelk through the mud." I could distinctly hear the ruffian lashing his tail within his shell as he replied: "It's all very well for you, old boy, but all that kind of nonsense you're talking don't come in here. If it were a question of saving your own life I'll bet you wouldn't give much ear to the whimperings of a sentimental blue point. Know then, old stick, that it isn't for the love of children that I am dragging this little brat along, but he's just going to be the supper of an old crab, who caught me this afternoon and only let me go on the condition that I found him something a little more toothsome and tender than I am."

'The cries of the infant were cruel to hear when it

THE WILD MAN

learnt the fate in store for it, and filled my heart with pity for the frail youngster. "Now come," said I to the whelk, "just wait a little while and consider, would it not always be a sad thing for you to reflect upon that you had been the cause of this frail young thing's death?" "Gammon!" answered the leather-hearted whelk, and proceeded on its journey. "Stay yet awhile," cried I, "and I will run and talk it over with the crab and see if his hard shell may hide a kinder heart than yours." "Well, look alive, old sentiments," replied the whelk; "it's a bit chilly waiting about out of the water when the tide's low. You'll see the old rascal over there by the sea."

'I hastened with what speed I might in the direction pointed out by the whelk, and presently came upon the old crab. Before I had time to greet him he accosted me with "Well, old kneebones, what's the trouble?" "No trouble of mine I do assure you," I replied as I seated myself by his side, taking care at the same time to keep well out of reach of his two pincer claws, that wobbled about wickedly in my direction; thus in some trepidation I continued the conversation. "The trouble is that of an innocent blue pointlet, now alas! in the toils of a perfect bully of a whelk, a worthless rough who is thus victimising the innocent to save himself from ending his paltry existence in your inside. Now my good fellow, I am perfectly certain that you are not going to allow this, indeed you are not the sort to sacrifice another's life

THE WILD MAN

to satisfy your own greed. Let me press you, just for once, to go supperless to bed, and thus assuage the anguish of a most affectionate mother."

'Much to my mortification and surprise, my conciliatory speech was met by roars of laughter from the flippant old crab. Peal upon peal disturbed the still evening air, and when the last clash of the hideous uproar had died away among the distant hills, the unfeeling brute, now in a state of collapse from loss of breath, gasped out:—"What, me give up the only chance of saving myself from that scoundrel of a lobster who only let me go on my promising to secure him something for supper a little less hard than myself! Well," continued the crab, "that's a good 'un, that is. My good chap you must be quite out of your senses. Why, not only will I hand over the baby oyster to the lobster, but I intend also to have my supper off that tough old idiot of a whelk, who reckons he's going to get off scot-free, and old mother blue point, too, if I can find her," and then, as an afterthought, "and you, old marrow-bones, wouldn't make half a bad tit-bit if I could get hold of you," and he made a horrid dash at me as he spoke. However, I easily evaded him, and from a safer distance argued the matter out with him in the following way :—

'"Allow me, my dear crustacean, to put the matter to you in this light. Now, first of all, clear your mind of all unnecessary bias. Suppose," said I, "that you

THE WILD MAN

AND KILLED IT ON THE SPOT

were to change places with the young oyster, suppose, we'll say, that you had the near prospect of being devoured by the greedy lobster. How would you feel, I say, if your neighbour not only refused to exert himself in any way to extricate you from your predicament, but also gloried in being the main cause of the disaster that threatened you?"

'The wily scoundrel merely replied, "Ask me another," and with his left eye-stalk bent towards the ground, insolently winked at me with the other. Despairing of penetrating his tough shell with kindly suggestions, I temporised with him, and succeeded in persuading him to desist from his evil intentions until I had talked it over with the lobster. Out of sheer perversity the crab directed me wrongly, but in good time, after some wandering here and there, I discovered the lobster.

'I pleaded my case to him as eloquently as I had already done to the others,—nay, even more eloquently, being, no doubt, a little more used to it by now, but yet with no apparent good result. The wary creature pretended ignorance. "To which crab do you refer?" said he, in a questioning tone; "I have so much business with crustaceans in one way and another that you would be surprised to learn how confused I become in my dealings with them." To the best of my ability I described the appearance of the old crab, and aided my description with a slight sketch on the sand made with the point of my umbrella. He gazed at this with much interest and murmured to himself "considerable artistic talent," and then aloud, "Oh yes, yes, I remember him quite well; indeed, he was here only recently about a little matter of supper. Well, well, I'm afraid I cannot be of any help to you here. You see, it's like this. Earlier in the day, I came to a little arrangement (quite a little business affair, by the way) with an old lady conger eel I have known for many years, and it happened in this way. We were having a little dispute as to who should sup off the other, and without going into details, the upshot of it all was that the eel managed to tie herself in a knot round my throat, and so, you see, was mistress of the situation. I need not tell you that I did not lose my presence of mind—indeed, I never do—and I politely asked her if she had ever tasted crab, and effectually persuaded her that they were much better eating than lobster, and undertook to procure her a beauty (thinking all the time, of course, of our mutual friend), on the understanding that I should go quite free. It's very sad and all that sort of thing, no doubt, about the little oyster—sweet little chuck—indeed, I am more sorry than I appear to be about it, but really what can one do?" And the lobster shrugged his bristling shoulders. "Speaking to you," he continued, "as one man of the world to another, business is business after all, you know. And if we don't fulfil our obligations, where do we stand? Of course, I don't say but what a little chat with the conger might make it all right, and there's no harm in trying—she's a nice eel. I feel sure you would like her, at least I felt I should, when I invited her to be my supper—and if nothing comes of the meeting, well, we shall none of us be any worse off than we are at the present moment. If at any other time I can be of use to you, I do hope that you will not hesitate to come round and ask. Good day."

'I now left him to search for the conger, whom I found dozing in a pool near the sea. I took her out and placed her gently on the sand, and she gradually opened her eyes and fastened them on me. I once more expounded the reasons why, in my opinion, this cruel arrangement should not be persisted in. I quite astonished myself by my own eloquence, which grew more impassioned as I proceeded, and noticed that the old conger seemed deeply impressed. As I came to the most affecting parts of my argument the expression in her eyes grew really tender, and at the mention of the little blue point a tear gathered in each eye and slowly coursed down her shiny form. At the conclusion of my appeal the conger drew in a deep breath and replied:—"Well, I never! Now that is what I really do call good and kind. Oh pray come and sit down beside me on the sand and tell me all about it—now do, and tell me what first put it into your head—it is so very nice to come across a little real sentiment in these matter-of-fact times." Without waiting for me to proceed she rattled on:— "Upon my word, you really must have the kindest heart in the world—but are you quite sure you are comfy? Why not come round the other side; you'll be out of the wind there, and we can talk it over without anything to interfere with us. I quite agree with you in everything you have said, and I must say that I know of nothing more delightful than to find one's own thoughts expressed so much more clearly than one could do it oneself. Do you know, I am quite delighted to have met you, and hope that this is the commencement of one of those lasting friendships. . . ."

'Thus she gabbled on, and thinking to myself, here, at last, is a kind-hearted soul, I asked her to promise to take the baby oyster back to its sorrowing mother, when she received it from the lobster. "What an extremely kind thought," she replied; "I assure you there is nothing in the whole world I would love to do so much as to take the little thing back to its Ma."

THE WILD MAN

WE COOKED ONE GREAT STEAK

Glancing dreamily at the sky the old eel continued:—
"Dear little mite! I can see it even now, in my mind's eye, as it skips to its mother; she, dear soul, the while shedding pearls of delight,—a memory to carry to your grave. But I expect you must be going now—no doubt you are as busy as the rest of us—are they all well at home?—good-bye," and she prepared to return to the sea. "But, my dear woman," I protested, "I have not yet received your promise to see the little oyster home." "Now," said the eel, "pray don't spoil the pleasant evening we have had—but never mind—don't look so serious—come round some evening

THE WILD MAN

with the wife and children—don't say you won't." "But, Madam," I answered, "I am waiting for your promise to see the little one home." "My dear Sir," she replied at last, growing rather red in the face, "I can give you nothing of the kind, and must really refer you to the whale who captured me a little while ago, and only released me because I promised to procure him a lobster, which I persuaded him would be much more digestible and less bilious than I should prove to be as a meal."

'I now went in search of the whale, whom I discovered disporting himself in the sea a very little way from the shore. Taking my shoes and stockings off, I waded as near to him as I dared, and to conciliate him right off I wore as benignant an expression as I could assume and thus addressed him: "Of one thing I am convinced," said I, "and it is that you are the last person in all the world who would willingly give pain to anything,—least of all to a baby oyster." "Quite so, quite so," snorted the whale, "and what is more I never have and, upon my soul, I never *will*." "Bravo, good resolution," cried I, and then in moving terms I explained the situation and urged him to take the blue pointlet back to its mother on receiving it from the conger eel. "What is this you say," roared the whale; "do you mean to tell me that in exchange for her own fat self that villainous conger-eel now offers me a baby oyster instead of the promised lobster? Is it for this gross insult that I allowed her to resume

THE WILD MAN

her wretched existence? Well, I'm thundered!" and the enraged monster leapt seventy feet into the air. "Where is she?" roared he, and made off in the direction of the conger.

'But the old girl was one too many for the whale this time, and having heard his remarks on her conduct, off she darted after the lobster, saying to herself that as the whole arrangement had fallen through, she might just as well sup off the lobster,—besides, the claws would stew up quite well for the children's dinner to-morrow. The lobster in his turn, seeing the conger approach, at once understood that the affair was all off and left his little cave by the back door as conger entered by the front, and made for the place where he knew he would find the crab, arguing to himself thus:—"At any rate, the crab will make an excellent supper to which I have every right; for after all, as I have before remarked, business is business, and he will certainly be unable to fulfil his obligations." The saucy crab, however, saw him coming along with his mouth wide open ready to gobble him up, and shouted tauntingly to him:—"Keep your bristles on, old prawn" and ran off after the whelk. "Nothing really matters," thought he, "and as I feel a bit peckish I may as well eat up friend whelk and the blue pointlet'll come in for a light breakfast in the morning." The cowardly whelk, reading the crab's evil intention in his eyes offered him the baby oyster. "Thanks, old flint," said the crab, "I'll have you first

179

and the youngster another time," and he pounced on the whelk and ate him right up. But as he was crawling off in great comfort the old lobster overtook him and in no time polished him off. The lobster, now too contented to move quickly, was slowly returning to the water when up came the conger-eel who, without any delay, proceeded to strangle him and then to gobble him up. After her feast, the old girl, in her turn, felt drowsy. "I think," said she, "I now deserve a nap," and she lay down in a pool and went fast asleep. Presently the whale came along, having been hunting for the conger all over the place. As soon as he caught sight of her he roared in his wrath, "Is this what you call keeping your bargain?" and with one gulp he bolted her,—head, fins, tail and all.

'Then, having accomplished his revenge, and at the same time satisfied his appetite, his contentment was complete and he rolled over on his side in the shallow water, and fell into a deep sleep.

'Now, thought I, is this not providential? Is there not here not merely the evening meal I left my cave to seek, but many meals for my good wife and children, —enough in fact to ward off hunger throughout the winter that is now fast approaching. Taking up a great rock I hurled it with all my force at the head of the whale and killed it on the spot. I now proceeded to cut up the great creature and carry it, piece by piece, to my cave, and that very night, when it was all

THE WILD MAN

safely stowed, we cooked one great steak for supper, waking the children in order that they might share the meal, and the remainder my good wife preserved in brine. Thus in comfort we lived the winter through.

'The little oyster found its way back to its mother, and so grateful were they both for my endeavours to help them, that they took up their abode with us. Bertram grew to a fine chubby blue point. "Just like his father," said the proud mother, and nothing reached our hearts so nearly as his playful, charming ways.'

THE MUSICIAN

THE MUSICIAN

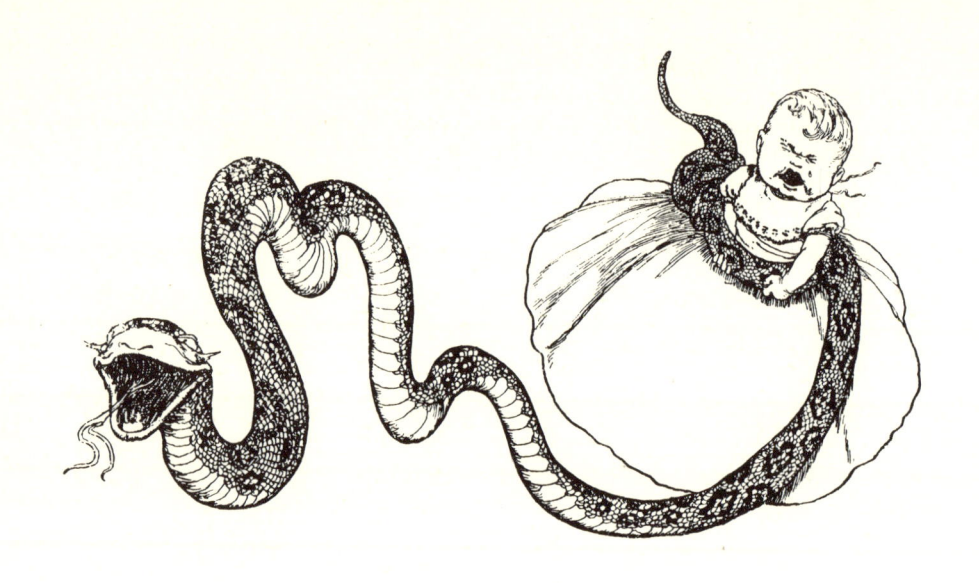

SOMETIMES now the old King showed signs of weariness, and Bill bethought him that a little music occasionally might soothe his nerves. So in the very next town they came to he engaged the only musician in the place, and very willing he was too to come along.

He played very wonderful music on his old concertina, often assisted with his voice, and one evening, after a very beautiful performance, the talented creature related the following story to his enchanted hearers:—

'Right glad have I been, good fellows all, to join you in this your noble enterprise to right our stout old brother of Troy here, and in good time I trust that

THE MUSICIAN

my great deeds shall prove my sincerity. But, in the meantime, as supper hour draws on apace, and the frizzling cutlets do scent the evening air, a little story should not be amiss to distract your anxious minds, and thus to check the impatience of your appetite.

'Know then, my jovial birds, my cunning blades, that I am the eldest son of that Prince of Polynesia who united the scattered kingdoms of this unwieldy archipelago into one vast empire, over which he ruled with even-handed justice and some common-sense until his death. Ah! lads, if all had their rights I should at the present moment be seated on the soft cushions of my father's throne, and maybe more able to be of help to you than I am now; but you must take the will for the deed.

'My word! what a plump and healthy child was I, and withal as jolly and as hearty as the day was long. Moreover, was not I the pride of the empire and the envy of all the other kings and princes who had ever seen or heard of me? Alas! who could have foretold that I was thus early in life destined to have a real good taste of the troubles of this weary world, and, though surrounded by every care and attention and the object of the greatest affection that ever bubbled in the human heart, shortly to become the victim of the meanest spite.

'But to proceed with the yarn—neither care nor expense was spared in my upbringing, to which possibly more thought was devoted than even to

THE MUSICIAN

the education of our very well-educated and trustworthy friend, the buxom Sicilian char-woman. At all events, the most certificated nurses procurable were continually being engaged, but apparently only to be dismissed again, for, almost perfect as most of them were, I can assure you that, in the course of a very little time they were certain, of course, to reveal (as was only natural) some slight weakness, and I ask you, good comrades all, which of us is without 'em? This overcarefulness on the part of my good parents was to be the cause of the disaster that was soon entirely to change the trend of my life.

'It came about in this way. One of the discharged nurses, indignant at what, with some show of reason, she considered an injustice to herself (she had been dismissed for curling my hair only a little to the right instead of quite to the right), resolved to revenge herself on her late master and mistress, in such a manner as should be most likely to leave them wretched for the remainder of their lives. Knowing the overextravagance of their affection for me, she cruelly determined to strike them in this, their weakest spot. One dark night, after cleverly evading the ever-wakeful guards, she crept into my father's palace. Stealing up the main staircase without attracting observation, she arrived at the now empty throne-room, which she stealthily traversed, keeping all the while close to the wall. She then passed through the little door at the left of the grand throne and found herself in the

THE MUSICIAN

billiard-room. She had not, however, taken two steps therein when a fearful panic seized her, for what should she behold but the stout form of my rare old dad the emperor leaning over the table, apparently in the act of making a brilliant stroke. A few seconds' consideration, however, served to convince the vengeful creature that he was fast asleep. Gnashing her teeth at the old gentleman, she hurried across the room and entered the library, in which my good mother was seated, reading. But so absorbed was the good lady in her book that she took no notice whatever of the agile intruder, as she entered by one door and swiftly left by the other. She now successively passed through the state ball-room, the music-room, the third best drawing-room, the second best ball-room, and the state bed-room, and mounting the back stairs, came to the suite of rooms occupied by the nurses, and eventually reached the nurses' dining-hall, into which my nursery led, without having excited any one's observation.

'Opening my door very quietly, she peeped in. All was dark inside except for the glimmer of a night-light which shone on the frilling of my cradle and on the form of the nurse then in office, who had fallen asleep over her supper of stewed apples. Creeping in quietly, the evil-minded woman lifted my sleeping form from the cradle, so gently that she did not awaken me, and, holding me closely to her, once more successfully passed through all the apartments she had already traversed, without arousing any suspicion, and at length found herself again in the open air.

'Without losing a moment, she now made off to the woods, and after wandering in these for some time, she met an old witch with whom, no doubt, she had an appointment. Seated on the grass, the two women haggled and haggled, and at last the treacherous nurse sold me to the witch for three cocoanuts, and then went on her way and out of my life for ever.

'Now it happened that the old witch lived in the hollow trunk of a tree with her foster son, a tiny gnome named Orpheus, as quaint a little object as ever I set eyes on, who played incessantly and most beautifully on an old concertina, the very one, in fact, which I now carry with me. The little fellow had been found some years before by the old witch wandering near the ruins of an old temple in the very middle of the wood. To whom he belonged, and whence he had come, no one knew,—not even he himself, perhaps. However, the old girl adopted him, and now nothing could exceed the motherly affection with which she regarded this dry and shrivelled-up little chap,— unless, indeed, it was the ardour with which the grateful gnome returned it. In fact, I learned some time afterwards that the old witch had purchased me solely that I might be a companion for this rum little person.

THE MUSICIAN

SHE NOW MADE OFF TO THE WOODS

'The old girl, weird as was her general appearance, did all she could to make me comfortable,—in fact far more than an ordinary witch would have dreamt of doing,—and in recognition of her well-intentioned attitude towards myself, I encouraged the spark of friendliness I began to feel for her. But for her darling son, as soon as I grew accustomed to his quaint appearance, and realised his kindness of heart and friendly disposition towards myself, I conceived a great affection. He would climb to the topmost branches of our tree, to practise his exercises every morning, in order that I should not be worried with melancholy

THE MUSICIAN

HE WOULD CLIMB TO THE TOPMOST BRANCHES

repetitions, and, when perfected in some melody, who shall describe the unaffected joy with which he would come down and play it for my delight? How often in the moonlight (I lying on the grass at his side) would he play over and over again to me some melancholy air, while our foster-mother, mayhap, would be sweeping the dead leaves from our abode, and preparing it for our night's repose.

'Not I alone was gratified and enchanted by his dulcet tones, for all the creatures of the woodland drew near and listened as night gradually covered the sky, and he played through his evening pieces.

'Elephants hovered around in the shadows of the trees, and sighed great slobbering sighs. Bullfinches, sparrows, eagles, flamingoes, wild geese, peacocks, turkeys, cranes, pelicans, and every manner of bird, thronged the branches of the trees, and, with their heads and beaks sunk almost into their feathers,

And played it for my delight

THE MUSICIAN

opened and closed their eyes in their rapturous surprise. The lions and tigers sprawled about, wishing, in pure shame at their habitual monstrous cruelties, that they had been vegetarians from the very beginning: such power had the music of Orpheus. Even the mad-headed monkeys and apes, sitting in rows amongst the trees, thought, Good heavens! what fools they were! and, blushing at their childish tricks, wondered if it yet were possible to reform and take a serious view of life. The old snake, quite overcome and enthralled by the delicious strains, opened wide his jaws, and allowed the little missel-thrush to nestle therein, and, thus protected from the night-air, to listen to the music in comfort. However, no lasting reformation was ever effected in their untamed natures, for no sooner had the music ceased than each scurried away, once again to resume his depredations and savage ways.

'It happened one evening that the gnome surpassed himself by his rendering of some enchanting melodies, and every one was quite enthralled and rendered almost helpless. The birds sank their heads and beaks lower and lower into their feathers, as the music proceeded, until they were no longer visible. The lions and tigers rolled on their backs in the grass, in an agony of despair at their own unreformable lives: the elephants turned quite white, and trembled so violently that they could hardly support their own huge bulks and leant against one another to prevent

THE MUSICIAN

themselves coming down with a crash; such a great lump had risen in the throat of the giraffe as quite distorted his otherwise graceful neck; while the monkeys gibbered and blubbered tearfully to themselves, and the old rascal of a snake slipped right off into a trance.

'At last the music ceased, and the little musician left me while he went in to hang up his musical instrument in safety. Meanwhile, in spite of the state to which they had been elevated, the absurd creatures had all scurried off, as usual, with no other thought in their savage minds than to get each his own supper at any cost. The old snake, however, did not recover as quickly as the others, and when at length he awakened from his trance, he could see that all the others had vanished, and that I was lying on the grass, quite unprotected, the gnome not having, as yet, returned to my side. "Ha, ha!" said he to himself, his savage nature having returned in all its force, "what a slice of luck! By gum! I never see such a beauty. Won't the youngsters be just delighted!" He rapidly slithered in my direction and, quickly tying the end of his long form securely round me, slithered away again, carrying me through the long grass at a bewildering speed.

'After travelling in this rough fashion for some time, we at length came to a clearing in the heart of the wood, in which stood all that remained of the ancient temple, and amongst its fallen columns and walls, overgrown as they were with wild flowers and tall grasses, the old snake had made his home, where

THE MUSICIAN

he lived in comfort with his wife and a large brood of pranksome snakelets.

'We were greeted by the youngsters with every mark of joy and surprise. "How good of you, Henry," cried the mother, "and what a really fine specimen! Shall we have him to-night, or keep him for next Tuesday, my birthday you know, dear?" After a little talk it was decided that I should be held over until the next Tuesday, and in the meantime I was placed in the larder, and given plenty of odd scraps to eat, no doubt to keep me plump and in good condition.

'Tuesday came round in due course and, in order to celebrate the day in a manner suitable to the greatness of the occasion, the old snake invited all his neighbours. When I was brought out of the larder, on a large dish, roars of delight rose to the sky from the throats of the assembled guests, all seated round on the fallen stones of the ruined temple.

'The old lion was there, smacking his lips in anticipation of a nice cut, and the tiger's mouth was visibly watering at the prospect of such a feast: while, as for the little snakelets, they kept up quite a clamour in their impatience to get at me. The monkeys, of course, contributed their share to the general uproar, though they seemed more inclined to fasten their eyes on the filberts and almonds with which I was garnished. The eagles took the whole thing very seriously and, flapping their great wings, screeched to the sky in their eagerness to begin; and all the other guests, the giraffes, the zebras, the hippos, the storks, the flamingoes, the wild cats, the pelicans, the wild geese, the peacocks, the turkeys, and every thinkable animal contributing to the general noise, there was such an awful din that the snake could only obtain silence by using the thin end of his long body as a flail on the drum-like sides of the elephant. He then made a few remarks on the importance of the occasion, and referred to his wife in quite a graceful way, for a snake; and, continuing, asked one of the guests to volunteer to carve. The stork, having a very convenient beak for the purpose, stood up and offered his services, which were gratefully accepted.

'I was now placed on the grass directly in front of the carver, who was about to skewer me with his long and sharp beak, when there came to our ears from far away amongst the trees that surrounded us on every side, the sweet harmonies of that lovely song "The Pond where Herbert Drownded," played with the greatest sympathy on the concertina. At once the stork turned its head in the direction whence the sound proceeded, and as it gradually drew nearer and nearer I became more and more convinced that such music could only be produced by my friend and foster-brother.

'All the creatures in varying degrees were affected; the snake and his wife coiled themselves on the grass and gasped in rapture; the stork and all the birds closed their eyes, and their heads sank lower and lower

THE MUSICIAN

SWEEPING THE DEAD LEAVES

into their fluffy bodies, until like balls of feathers they rolled over and lay trembling in the grass.

'The lion and tiger were so overcome that they leant their old heads on their paws and sobbed aloud, while the monkeys grew fidgety and quite self-conscious at first, and then abandoned themselves to the melancholy aroused by the music.

'The gnome, whom I afterwards learnt had been wandering about the wood playing mournful airs on his concertina ever since he had missed me, now drew near, and finishing "The Pond where Herbert Drownded" proceeded with "Poor Molly Dawson" and other tunes of an equally affecting nature. On seeing that all were sufficiently bowled over, he struck up with "Oh, Jack, he was a Bright Spark," and so lively and brisk was the measure that up they all jumped and danced and danced with the greatest spirit.

'The strangest figure of all was cut by the old snake who pirouetted on the end of his tail at the greatest speed, in which weird performance he was soon joined by his wife. The eagle extended his wings and waltzed with the elephant; the lion and tiger spun round, holding each other by the paw, so quickly that it was almost impossible to see them; the old turtle rolled over on the back of its shell and span like a teetotum, with the silly monkeys linking hands and in one wide ring skipping around it; in fact, all got up and jumped and lumped and sprawled about in the most ridiculous fashion until they were quite out of breath. Nevertheless, Orpheus would not let them rest, but marched off playing the most exciting music, and all the infatuated creatures, quite forgetful of their banquet, followed him through the wood. Strange enough, in all conscience, was this, but how much stranger by far was it when the very stones of the ruin leapt up, and rolling over and over, also followed in this odd procession as it tramped and crashed through the trees.

'From where I was seated on the dish I could hear the sounds of the music gradually fading away, as the musician led the noisy crew further and further

THE MUSICIAN

WITH NO OTHER WEALTH THAN MY CONCERTINA

off; the crash of the falling branches and the crackle of the breaking underwood died down in the distance and I knew that I was saved.

'The little gnome led the bewitched creatures such a dance through the wood that one by one they fell down in a state of collapse, and when the last was quite overcome, the faithful fellow returned to the temple and carried me home.

'Never again did they leave me alone for a single second until I was able to take care of myself, and I spent the years of my boyhood in great happiness with these two simple and kindly souls. Brother Orpheus took no end of pains in teaching me to play the

THE MUSICIAN

concertina and, eager to learn, I soon became proficient. But, dear lads, clever as you know me to be, never could I even approach the skill of my good and patient master.

'In the course of time the old witch had to die, and the grief of her little foster son was so great at his loss that, try as I would, I could not in any way lighten it. One day soon after I missed the little man, and he never returned again. All that he left behind him for me to remember him by was his old concertina.

'I waited by the tree for many a long day, still thinking that he would return, until I was compelled at last to abandon all hope of ever seeing him again. I wandered out into the world with no other wealth than my concertina, but how often since have I had to bless the memory of my little friend who thus endowed me with the means of subsistence, and, at the same time, with a protection against all manner of evil.'

THE LOST GROCER

THE LOST GROCER

FOR many and many a weary mile the persevering little band had now trudged on without meeting with any adventure worth relating, and every one was longing for the end of their travels, when one lovely evening they came across a good-natured-looking policeman, fast asleep on a stile by the roadside. The tramp, tramp of the army awakened him, and with a gentle smile he got off his perch and walked alongside the King. Charmed with his easy manner, the King jokingly asked him of what he had been dreaming that he smiled so pleasantly. 'Oh, of old times and old friends,' the policeman replied, and then as he walked along he thus related the strangest of experiences :—

'Many years ago it was my happy lot to be the

principal policeman of the pleasant little town of Troutpeg, situated, as you know, on the banks of the river Peg, just where it flows into the estuary of the Drip, that here broadens into that well-known land-locked harbour of the same name, and thus finally finds its way to the sea. Nestling amongst its stone-capped hills, the happy place seemed designed by a kind nature as a retreat for all who were blithe and amiable, and such indeed it proved to be, for no more kindly and genial souls than the Troutpegsters could be found. Their simplicity was delightful, though perhaps such as to incline them all the more readily to believe in the wild legends of the country-side. Many were the strange stories told by the shepherds, who tended their flocks on the hills at night, of wild rites, and uncouth dances performed by ghostly beings, in the light of the moon, amidst the ancient circles of Druid stones. Little else, however, was there to disturb the peaceful thoughts of the Troutpegsters.

'The prosperity of the township was so great, and the comfort of each of its inhabitants so well assured that for many years no wickedness of any kind had shown its head, and the life of a policeman in this happy and secluded town was one long summer holiday. To be sure, a little skirmish here and there amongst the lads might make it wise gently to exert my authority, or a little quarrel amongst the girls call forth a slight rebuke, but otherwise my life was one of unbroken peace.

THE LOST GROCER

'My dearest friend was the tea-grocer, a man of sad and dreamy ways and quite devoid of guile, who returned my affection with all the ardour of a singularly loving nature. He shared his every joy with me, and when his holidays came round no greater recreation could he find than in my society. Walking by my side as I strolled along my beat, he would confide to me his simple hopes and fears, and in his troubles seek my readily extended sympathy. Such simplicity and inoffensive mien had he as brought to him a rich harvest of respect and love, together with the custom of his fellow-townsmen.

'In time his little store became quite an evening resort for those older townsmen who, no longer able to race about the green when work was done, would perhaps look in to purchase half a pound of coffee or tea, or sugar or salt for the good wife, and stay chatting with the amiable grocer. Then maybe one would look in to buy an ounce of tobacco, or the excellent snuff for which the grocer was far famed, and so on and so on until the shop was full. Seated around on the tea-chests, coffee bins, tobacco boxes and snuff tins, many a pleasant evening have we spent, enlivened by good-natured arguments and discussions on every conceivable subject.

'One sultry summer's afternoon, as I was standing thinking in the cobbled high-street, the quiet of the still warm day disturbed only by the gentle breathing of the shopmen as they dozed amongst their wares,

THE LOST GROCER

or the distant bleating of the sheep as they browsed in and out the rocks and Druid stones capping the surrounding hills, the comforting remembrance came to me of many a refreshing cup of tea partaken with the grocer in the snug little parlour behind his shop. With hardly a thought of what I was about, I allowed my idle steps gently to stray towards the homely store of my friend. Entering therein, and finding that he was away from home, I sat me down upon the little chair, so thoughtfully provided for weary customers, and with my head supported by the counter, resumed my broken train of thought until, completely overcome by a sense of drowsy comfort, I feel asleep.

'I was suddenly awakened by the church clock striking eight, and found that all the town was wrapped in slumber and that the grocer had not yet returned. Wondering what on earth could keep him away so late, and hoping that no harm had overtaken him, I stiffly arose from my seat, stretched myself, and betook me to my home and bed.

'On the following morning my first thought was for my friend, and on learning that he had not returned during the night, I called in turn on each of his neighbours,—the doctor, the vicar, the solicitor, the postman, and the corn-chandler, and many another equally interested in his movements. Not one, however, had seen him since the previous day, and all showed the liveliest concern and anxiety at his mysterious absence.

THE LOST GROCER

'Night followed day, and day again followed night, with no sign of the vanished grocer. Weeks now passed by, and grief took possession of the little town at the loss of one who was missed at every turn. Hoping that even yet he might return, we kept his shop still open for him, and the little birds, encouraged by the silence, flew in and out and nested in the scales and amongst the stores, glutting their fluffy little bodies with the sugar-plums, the currants, the herbs and spices that everywhere abounded. And even the swallows, so much entertainment did they find therein, forgot, as the summer drew to its close, to fly away, preferring much to sleep the winter through in comfort.

'But alas! months, and years and years and years rolled by, and the grocer never returned, and in time little enough thought was given to one who had, at one time, been held in such esteem by all. But we, the older Troutpegsters, still thought at times of our vanished friend, and many were the theories we suggested to account for his disappearance.

'One held that he had been beguiled by gypsies, another that he had been stolen to be exhibited as a rare model of virtue in some distant clime, while others believed that the fairies, envious of our happiness in possessing such a friend, had taken him from our midst; but all agreed that we should have guarded our treasure with greater care.

'One never-to-be-forgotten evening the doctor, the

THE LOST GROCER

AFFECTED BY HIS STORY

solicitor, the vicar, the corn-chandler, and myself (some of us already stricken in years) were seated, as was now our evening custom, upon the rustic bridge that carries the road across the river Peg. The fragrant smoke of our long pipes rising to the evening sky, our conversation, as was now so frequently the case, had drifted from politics, sport, fashions and the latest police intelligence to lovingly-recalled memories of our long-lost friend, and so sad did we become that lumps as large as egg plums rose to our throats, and our eyes brimmed over with tears.

'Drying our eyes we now smoked on in silent contemplation of the past; the night gradually drew down, and the first star appeared in the cloudless sky when there came to us the sound of a distant footstep, coming along the road towards the town, and presently a strange figure hove in sight,—an old, old man, with

THE LOST GROCER

PLUMP INTO THE RIVER WE WENT

long tangled grey hair and shaggy beard, clothed in the most pitiable rags, torn, and held together with straw and odd pieces of string. He passed slowly across the bridge, leaning heavily on his staff, and limped with difficulty towards the town, into which with one accord we followed him.

'Down the cobbled high street he walked until he came to the shop of the vanished grocer into which he turned without any hesitation. Wondering what business could take him there, we all hastened to the door of the shop, and there, with the utmost astonishment, beheld the stranger remove his threadbare coat, and replace it with the grocer's moth-eaten apron that had hung for so long from a peg on the door; then he commenced dusting the shop and putting it

THE LOST GROCER

straight. As I gazed, my astonishment gave place to the most incredulous amazement when I detected in the old man a fancied likeness to the departed grocer. At last, after closer scrutiny, I was convinced that it was indeed no other than my friend actually returned after all these years, and as he at the same time more easily recognised me, we fell into each other's arms, and who shall describe the extravagance of our joy?

'In a little while, when we had calmed down, we all retired to the little parlour behind the shop, and our good friend brewed us a cup of tea as of old, and after a little gentle persuasion related to us the following strange story of his disappearance:—

'"On that memorable summer afternoon, many years ago, as I was weighing out the sugar into pound and half-pound packets (which, as you may remember, was my rule at that time of day to prepare for the evening trade), a strange old gentleman, clothed in the deepest black from cap to slippers, yet withal possessed of the most snowy ringlets and beard, entered my shop and begged of me some food for his family, assuring me that they were all slowly dying of starvation.

'"Affected by his story, I was making up for him a parcel containing lentils, raisins, dates, figs, sugar, and other goods which I thought might be acceptable, when, to my astonishment, the ungrateful old rascal snatched up a large tin of the finest snuff, which you will remember I used to sell in great quantities, and bolted with it out of the shop.

'"Without a moment's hesitation I divested myself of my apron, and donning my coat, followed him at the greatest speed. Away he ran down the high street towards the bridge, which he very soon crossed, and now along the river bends he sped, with me close at his heels. For miles we ran, even as far as the source of the river Peg, which we doubled and came tearing down the other side. I now perceived that, in spite of his age, he ran almost quicker than I did. Presently into the river he plunged, I following close, and then he retraced his steps towards its source. Once more plump into the river we went, and as I scrambled up the opposite bank I noticed to my dismay that, while I grew more tired and out of breath as we ran, he became brisker and fresher. Discarding his hat, cloak, and slippers, though still holding on to the snuff tin, he now appeared in robes of dazzling white, which, with his hair and long white beard, flowed behind him as he ran, and gradually increased the distance between us.

'"Soon I could perceive that he was making for the hill above the town which, with no difficulty at all, he mounted long before I had reached its foot, and when at last I struggled to the top the old rogue was seated upon one of the Druid stones that here in one great circle crown the hill, smiling, and hugging to himself the while the tin of snuff. On seeing me

Followed him at the greatest speed

THE LOST GROCER

TpHERE GREW IN FRONT OF ME A GREAT MOUND

again, he soon jumped down, and I dodged him in and out of the stones for at least three hours by the church clock, and then weary and utterly dejected I sat me down on a stone in the centre of the ring and wept bitterly. Directly beneath me I could see, through my tears, the lights of our little town shine out here and there from the gathering darkness, while over the hills, away to my left, the edge of the full red moon began to show. As higher and higher it climbed the sky, one by one there leapt from the earth beneath each stone an aged Druid all clothed in white, with long waving grey locks and beard, and crowned with garlands of oak leaves, holly, laurels, and mistletoe. When the circle of Druids was quite complete the old rascal who had lured me from my shop, and who now appeared to be their chief, stepped towards me, now far too bewildered and astounded to resist, and solemnly placed upon my brow a wreath of wild violets. Then separately, each of the Druids came forward with

THE LOST GROCER

some offering which he placed before me, afterwards returning to his place in the circle, so that presently there grew upon the grass in front of me a great mound of vegetables, fruit, flowers, haunches of venison, fowls, hares, rabbits, and young lambs. At length, every Druid having made his offering, their chief handed round the tin of snuff from which each old fellow took a large pinch, and then, linking hands, they danced wildly round me.

'" In utter silence, by the light of the moon, now high in the sky, these solemn rites were performed, and still without a sound they whirled quicker and quicker around me, their feet hardly seeming to touch the ground, and their long loose garments streaming after them as they flew.

'" Presently the distant chime of the church clock striking twelve reached me from the town below and I gradually fell into a trance, as one by one the old Druids sank into the earth beneath the stones.

'" Every day since then until to-day have I passed in complete oblivion, and every night have I awakened to find myself seated on the stone in the centre of the ring of Druids, with all the power of resistance taken from me, compelled to be the object of their weird rites.

'" Last night, however, just as the church clock began to strike twelve, such a rush of memories flooded my brain, and such a longing to see my old home and friends took possession of me, that a

THE LOST GROCER

SNEEZING AND SNEEZING

terrible rage at the cruel tyranny of the Druids had gathered in my bosom before the clock had finished striking the hour. When it was about to strike the last beat, I arose from my seat in the centre of the circle and approaching the wicked old chief, I snatched the snuff tin from his hands and clapped it, snuff and all, right down over his eyes. Strange to say the contents of the tin had not diminished by so much as a single pinch, and such a fit of sneezing seized the old scoundrel that he rolled on the grass in the greatest distress, quite unable to put the usual spell upon me. All the other Druids, with abject terror expressed on their faces, sank at once into the ground. The form of the head Druid, sneezing and sneezing and sneezing, gradually faded away before my eyes, and long after he had completely disappeared the sneezing could still be heard. Eventually this died away, and pulling my clothes together as best I could (for by now they were all in rags), I made the best of my way home."

'Having finished his story the grocer now became very thoughtful, and we all sat round his little room smoking in silence until far into the night, wondering at the strange events he had related. Next day, and for a whole week, great festivities were held to celebrate his return, and the Mayor very willingly resigned his office in favour of one who was held in such esteem. Innumerable presentations were made to him and addresses read to him, yet, in spite of all the honours he received, never did he forget his old friends. Nor was he too proud to serve in his little shop, now enlivened by the songs of the birds he had not the heart to turn away. He spent the remainder of his useful life in the performance of kind deeds and in well-deserved happiness.'

THE MERCHANT'S WIFE

AND THE
MERCHANT

THE MERCHANT'S WIFE AND THE MERCHANT

'VERY, very good, indeed,' the King remarked when the policeman had finished his story, and he was so pleased that he gave all the youngsters a half-holiday, with strict injunctions to be back in time for tea.

THE MERCHANT'S WIFE

At tea-time they all came skipping back, bringing with them a little old man they had found, apparently lost, and moping about the common. He carried in front of him a pedlar's tray, on which were exposed for sale many little oddments, such as reels of cotton, needles, pins, ribbons, and even little toys, which he now hawked round amongst the assembled company. As many as were able bought some small thing or other out of kindness to the little merchant, and the good-natured old monarch invited him to tea.

While they were all enjoying this meal, they were disturbed by a great noise, very much like the galloping of a horse, and suddenly, without any warning, right into their midst there leapt a very large woman, who immediately seized upon the little merchant, and attempted to drag him away. Bill at once went to the assistance of the little fellow, and endeavoured to pacify his assailant. At length the irate creature calmed down, and addressing the company in an aggrieved tone, said:—'It's all very well for you people to stand up for this wicked man, but not one of you knows the dance the little wretch has led me for the last fifteen years.'

'Of course,' the King answered, 'it is hardly to be expected that we should know anything of either of you, considering that this is the very first time we have had the pleasure of meeting you. Perhaps you will be so kind as to enlighten us, and explain to us your strange conduct.'

THE MERCHANT'S WIFE

The large woman now sat down upon the grass and said:—'Well, I suppose I had better do so. Give me a cup of tea, and I'll let you know all there is to know.'

A cup of tea was accordingly handed to her, from which she took a sip, and then proceeded thus:—

'About fifteen years ago I was so unfortunate as to wed this poor specimen of a man you see before you, and we had not set up house together very long before I could see that he wanted thoroughly looking after, and, indeed, that he could hardly be allowed out by himself. Now this was very awkward, as his business required that he should be out all day, so I proposed to accompany him on his rounds. Holding him securely fastened to the end of a long cord, I never let him out of my sight for more than a minute at a time, and so kept him from mischief. After a year or so, however, this grew rather tiresome for me, as I had to neglect my household duties in attending upon my husband, and, in the end, was compelled to let him out again alone.

'But you may be sure I did not do this until I had laid down certain fixed rules for his behaviour, which I made him promise to obey. Amongst these, one was that he should start from home not a minute earlier and not a minute later than eight o'clock in the morning; another was, that if he returned either a minute earlier or a minute later than eight o'clock in the evening, he should go supperless to bed. And, would

Bringing with them a little old man

THE MERCHANT'S WIFE

you believe me, in spite of all my care, he would sometimes return earlier and, as I learnt afterwards, remain outside until the clock struck eight, when he would creep in as though he had only just returned?

'But my great trouble only began a few weeks ago, when, one evening, having cooked his nightly turnip, I waited patiently for my good man's return. At length the clock struck eight, and, to my surprise, it was not immediately followed by my husband's timid knock. One minute passed; two minutes passed; three minutes passed; four minutes passed; and, on the fifth minute, there was a low knock at the door, and in crept the miserable man, and cowered to his place. But, as you may suppose, there was no turnip for him *that* night, until he had given a satisfactory explanation of his late return. The only excuse the frightened little ruffian had to offer was, that he had dropped a needle on the road, and had to return for it. So he went supperless to bed.

'The next evening, having warmed up the old turnip, I again awaited his return. Eight o'clock struck, and, to my even greater surprise, it was not followed by the merchant's knock, and this time it was six minutes past before he entered, and with no better excuse for his late arrival than that he had dropped a reel of cotton on the road, and had to return for it. "Let this be a lesson to you, my man," said I, as I once more put away the turnip, which he had been regarding with longing eyes, and sent him to bed.

THE MERCHANT'S WIFE

'For the third time, on the following evening, I warmed up the turnip, feeling convinced that after the severe lesson he had received, my merchant would not again serve me such a trick. But eight o'clock struck, and then one minute passed; then two, three, four, five, six, seven, eight, nine, and as the minute-hand pointed to the ten, he crawled in on hands and knees, not daring to raise his eyes from the ground. And then I told him what I thought of his conduct.

'Without waiting to hear a word of explanation, I now locked him in a cupboard beneath the stairs, put the turnip away, and went to bed. In the morning I let him out, but of course gave him no breakfast, and in due time he took his tray of goods, and left the house without a word. Hardly had he departed three minutes. when I hastily donned my bonnet and shawl, and followed him, determined to learn, if possible, what had delayed him on the three previous evenings. Keeping at a safe distance, I followed him all over the town, but nothing unusual happened. He called at every house, displaying his wares to any one likely to buy; selling a ribbon here, perhaps some pins or needles there, but his conduct, on the whole, seemed harmless enough. At length the day passed by, and the merchant started homewards; but he had not moved many paces, when he came to a stop, and seemed to debate in his mind whether he should return or not. Then, looking up and down the road, and seeing no one watching him, he suddenly took to

THE MERCHANT'S WIFE

MOPING ABOUT THE COMMON

his heels, and ran as hard as he could in the opposite direction. I lost no time in climbing over the wall, behind which I had been hiding, and quickly followed him. Out of the town the villain ran as swiftly as he could go, and I followed as close as possible, without being seen by him, and was only just in time to see the rogue climb into an old barrel that was standing, end up, in a field near the roadway. "Now," thought I, "I've got you in a trap, my fine fellow," and I ran up to the barrel. I could hardly believe the evidence of my eyes when I found it to be quite empty. Amazed

THE MERCHANT'S WIFE

beyond measure, I at last turned my steps towards home.

'On arriving home, I found that my husband had not returned, and it was fully twenty minutes past eight when at last he appeared, but I was so astonished that I could not say a word to the little rascal, and once more he went supperless to bed.

'For four more days I followed the little man without approaching a solution to this riddle. Each day he would go about his business in the usual manner and, in the evening, he would run to the barrel, into which he would speedily disappear. He came home later and later every night, until I could stand this state of things no longer; and, on the sixth day I determined never to return until I had satisfactorily cleared up this mystery. This time, instead of following my merchant through the town, I went direct to the barrel, and, hiding myself behind a bush near by, prepared to wait there all day and see what happened.

'I had not made myself comfortable many minutes before I saw two old men coming along the road from the town; so old were they indeed, that they could only creep along by leaning one against the other. Right up to the barrel they crawled, and then, to my surprise, they scrambled over its sides and disappeared. Presently two more just as old and decrepit came along and disappeared in the same way. Now three more came, then two again, and then only one, all as old and wretched as could be, and each

THE MERCHANT'S WIFE

one crawled into the barrel and vanished. This went on for some time when, unable to restrain my curiosity and wondering why on earth the barrel didn't become full, I hurriedly left my hiding-place and looked therein, to find that it yet remained quite empty. I had barely time enough to regain my hiding-place when more and more old men came along the road and disappeared into the barrel.

'This went on all day, and when the evening drew near, I could see my little man approaching from the town. As I expected, he walked straight up to the barrel, and in a twinkling had vanished inside. Without giving myself a moment to think, I once more left my hiding-place and climbed into the mysterious old tub. It was certainly rather a tight fit, but I managed to get in somehow or other. Presently I was astonished and alarmed to find that the bottom of the barrel, which I had imagined to rest on the earth, began to give way and open like a trap-door, and I felt myself sinking lower and lower, down a sort of well. The next thing, I found myself at the bottom of the well, and at the mouth of a tunnel so narrow and low that I could only go through it on my hands and knees. This, however, I proceeded to do, and found that it opened into a great chamber cut out of the solid rock.

'Not daring to enter, I gazed into this strange place, which was lighted with many candles all affixed to the rocky walls with their own tallow. On the centre of the floor was piled a great heap of children's toys,—tin trumpets, wooden horses, drums, hoops, skipping-ropes, rocking-horses, peg-tops, in fact, every conceivable toy that a sensible child could wish for. Around this great heap, instead of children, sat all the poor miserable old men I had seen enter the barrel, and amongst them I now perceived my husband, who certainly seemed no happier than the rest. Securely hidden in the narrow passage from every one in the room, I could now watch all that took place, in the greatest comfort.

'Not a word was said by any of the decrepit creatures as they stared absently at the toys in the middle of the room. Presently one whom I took to be their host, as I had not seen him enter the barrel, took from a peg on the wall, from which it had been suspended by a piece of string, an old bent tin pipe and proceeded to play. At once the wrinkled faces of the poor old fellows began to brighten up, and as the music grew more lively, they rocked their withered frames to and fro to the tunes. Soon, one by one, they stood upon their feet, and seeming to lose their old age as the music every moment became more enchanting, they forgot their feebleness and danced gaily about the room.

'Younger and younger they grew, until my husband appeared to be such a dapper and bright little man that I could not prevent myself from leaving my hiding-place and going up to him and clasping him round the waist. Not a bit surprised did he seem to

THE MERCHANT'S WIFE

KEPT HIM OUT OF MISCHIEF

see me there, and as we danced merrily up and down the room, to my great joy and astonishment, I felt myself growing younger every moment, whilst the rest of the company, now all transformed to fine young men, danced in one circle round us, as handsome a couple as you would wish to see.

'Still the magical music continued, and if anything grew more and more enchanting as we grew younger and younger, until we seemed to be frolicsome boys

THE MERCHANT'S WIFE

GLORIOUS TARTS AND SWEETS

and girls once more. At last we found ourselves to be a crowd of little toddling children, and, my word! how we grabbed at the great heap of toys placed there for our amusement, and what a time we had to be sure!

'Under the great heap of toys, we discovered the most glorious tarts, pastries, cakes and sweets, and it didn't seem to matter how much you ate of them, for you never lost your appetite for more. At last, alas! the wonderful music quieted down, and by degrees we once more lost our childhood, then our youth, and, when the music suddenly stopped, we all returned to our old selves again, and fell flat on our faces quite tired out, while our host hung up his old tin pipe on its peg in the wall.

'When we had all somewhat recovered, I fixed my eye upon my husband. "Now," thought I, "I've got you. This is how you waste your time, is it? And why you come home late for supper." The conscience-

THE MERCHANT'S WIFE

IT DIDN'T MATTER HOW MUCH YOU ATE

stricken creature trembled before my gaze, and then made a rush for the door. All made way for him, but I quickly followed through the tunnel and mounted a ladder which led to the trap-door at the bottom of the barrel, out of which I climbed, but only in time to see the rascal disappear into the town. I then made the best of my way home.

'He had not returned when I arrived, so I waited three whole days and nights, prepared to make the unnatural man feel to the full my resentment at his shameful conduct. On the fourth day, as he had not come home, I went back to the tub, and not seeing any sign of him, I gave a kick to the old thing and sent it rolling over and over on its side. Would you believe me, there was not the slightest trace of any passage or well ever having existed beneath it. Since then I have wandered all over the country in search of this ungrateful wretch.' And the indignant woman, having finished her story, once more

THE MERCHANT'S WIFE

attempted to drag the affrighted little merchant away. Bill again intervened, and after a few very kind words, successfully persuaded her to allow her husband to remain with them, at the same time inviting her to make one of their brave band.

This she only consented to do on condition that the policeman also never left them, 'as you never know,' said she, 'what the little wretch will be up to next.'

The policeman having no objection to fall in with her wishes, they all marched on in peace.

THE CAMP-FOLLOWERS

THE CAMP-FOLLOWERS

TIME was now getting on, and the fidgety old King, weary of being constantly on the move, became more and more impatient to reach his journey's end. For many days they had been

THE CAMP-FOLLOWERS

crossing the great desert, and were fast approaching the further side when, one evening, the aggravating old fellow decided that they should march on right through the night. In vain did Bill point out to him how tired they all were; the old King would not even listen to him, so, whether they liked it or not, they had to jog on.

Wearily they trudged along, and towards morning they came upon a great stone sphinx, in the arms of which there nestled a company of little children, every one of whom was fast asleep. Presently, as the sun rose and shone under the lids of their eyes, they, one by one, awakened, and stared in mute astonishment at the dusty figures before them. Assuring them that they had nothing to fear at their hands, Bill, with the King's permission, invited them all to breakfast. Seated in a great circle on the sands, beneath the old sphinx, every one did his utmost to make the strangers comfortable and to remove their natural shyness; and, in a little while, it was a very jovial party that sat demolishing the substantial breakfast prepared for them. Many songs were sung and stories told by Bill and his comrades, and presently one of the little fellows, who appeared to be the youngest of their new friends, stood up and related the following story:—

'We are all brothers and sisters, and lived, until yesterday, with our good parents upon a sandbank in the mouth of the river Blim which, as you know, is one of the smaller tributaries of the river Nile. Our father

THE CAMP-FOLLOWERS

was a fisherman, and upon the only spot on the bank which remained invariably high and dry, the clever man had erected a shed which served us for home, and which, at least, protected us from the showers of spray blown from the rough seas, and the chill winds that blew across the neighbouring marshes, as well as the cold rains that, in the fall of the year, flooded the adjacent country for miles around. A dozen stout beams, that had been cast up by the waves, served, each with one end deeply embedded in the wet sand, as a framework for our humble mansion. These were covered over with numerous skins of fish and pieces of old rag, all neatly stitched together by our industrious mother, or pinned by fish-bones skilfully sharpened by grinding their ends between two stones. Our good dad's stock-in-trade consisted of one long piece of frayed string, with a sharpened fishbone, bent in the form of a hook, fastened at one end, a small boat and a paddle, the former of which he had skilfully fashioned out of an old basket that had been washed ashore, and over which he had stretched more of the rags and fish-skins, of which we always possessed a goodly supply saved over from our meals.

'During the long winter months we were entirely cut off from our fellow creatures by the floods and the terrible storms at sea, and were compelled to subsist entirely upon our own resources; and thus we learnt, after many a bitter trial, to make almost everything we required from the spoils brought home by our

They came upon a great stone sphinx

THE CAMP-FOLLOWERS

hard-working father. The flesh of the fish, of course, served us for meat, either fresh or pickled in brine, and then dried in the sun. The roes, prepared in the same way, were our only delicacies, and, by an indulgence in these, we used to celebrate our many birthdays. Fish dripping we had in plenty, and the bones were dried and ground between two rocks, making the finest flour for bread and pies. The tails and fins were always saved, and, after a simple drying process, made excellent fuel, easily set alight with sparks kindled by knocking two stones sharply together. A fine black ash was left from fires kindled in this way, which, mixed with a little sea-water, made one of the purest inks. The good dad always encouraged us to make notes on the smooth white skins of the young dab, bleached and dried in the sun, explaining how useful they would be to us in after-life, and showed us how to cut pens from the larger bones of the fish. The only parts which the unselfish man reserved for himself were the eyes which, when dried, were his only substitute for tobacco in that lone part of the world, and which he smoked in a pipe most beautifully carved by himself, from the spine of an old cod.

'The heads of the fish served the younger children for bricks, or even, after a little trimming, for dolls, with which they amused themselves during the long winter evenings. Many another device had we whereby we made the most of our very small opportunities, but you will readily see how dependent we were for everything upon the good fortune and resources of our father, without whom we should all very quickly have perished.

'For many days and nights at a time our good dad would remain upon the sea, returning sometimes with a good supply of fish; at other times, alas! with only one or two little dabs, or even with nothing at all. Yet, by dint of saving up for a rainy day, when we had more than enough for our present needs, we managed to jog along fairly comfortably. One sad winter's evening, however, our good parent returned, having caught nothing but a very small dab and a very severe cold. Our anxious mother, in a state of alarm, lit a great fire and, after making him take a bowl of steaming fish gruel, with his feet at the same time in a bath of hot sea-water, she sent him to bed, and covered him up with as many fish skins as she could spare from the house. The next day he was decidedly worse, and our anxiety increased day by day as he showed no signs of improvement. Very soon, with no one to replenish our larder, our stores began to run low, and starvation stared us in the face.

'At last one morning the invalid called our eldest brother to him and said to him:—"Son, our stores are all eaten up, and unless we obtain food by to-morrow morning we shall all surely die, so take my boat and fishing-line and see what luck will attend you." With tears in his eyes, the good-hearted boy left the house and very soon embarked.

THE CAMP-FOLLOWERS

THE HEADS SERVED FOR DOLLS

'Having paddled some way out to sea, he threw his line, and fished and fished. After a little while he drew it in again to find, alas! that he had caught nothing. For the second time he cast his line, and fished and fished and fished, but on again pulling in the line he found that he had no better luck. He now for the third time threw out his line, and fished and fished and fished and fished, yet no better fortune attended him; so, bitterly disappointed, he wound up the tackle and paddled home.

'Sorrowfully the unhappy father heard of his eldest son's want of success, and then sent for his second

233

THE CAMP-FOLLOWERS

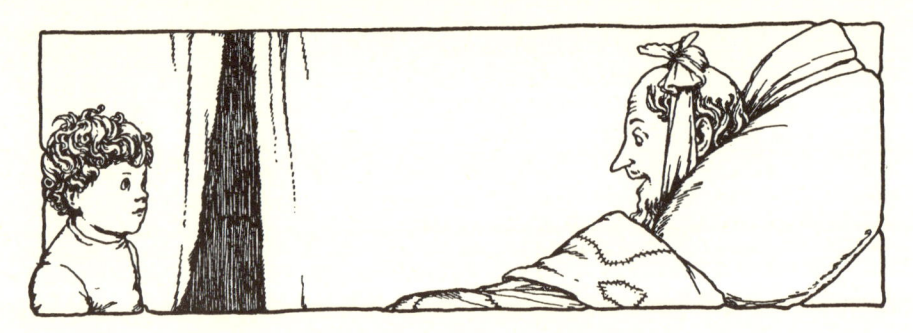

YOU ARE NOW OUR ONLY HOPE

eldest son, and requested him to see if fortune would be kinder to him than it had been to his brother. But, alas! he returned likewise without even so much as a whitebait. Then, one after the other, he sent all his sons except myself, who am the youngest of all, but not a little piece of luck awaited any of them. The wretched man now called me to him and said:—"Son, hitherto I have been reluctant to send one so young upon such an errand, but, alack-a-day! you are now our only hope; unless good fortune waits upon you we shall all perish."

'After comforting him as much as I could, and assuring him that I would do my best, I hastened down to the shore and embarked in the little boat. I paddled a good way out to sea until I came to a suitable fishing-ground, and then threw out my line. I fished and fished and fished and fished, and on drawing in my line found nothing on the hook except the bait, a wretched piece of dried fish skin, which looked very draggled as it rose from the water.

THE CAMP-FOLLOWERS

"Better luck next time," thought I, as I threw my line for the second time, and fished and fished and fished and fished and fished. Yet, on pulling up the line, I found to my dismay that instead of better luck I had even worse, if that were possible, for the wretched bait had vanished from the hook. "Once more," thought I, as I dropped my line overboard for the third time, "and, fish or no fish, I must give it up, even though we all die of starvation." So I fished and fished and fished and fished and fished with all my might, and when at length I had hauled it in you may imagine my distress when I discovered that not merely was there no fish upon the line, but that the hook itself had disappeared. With tears of rage and disappointment I now gave it up and prepared to return, but I had not gone very far when I thought, "Shall I have just one more try even without hook or bait?" And not giving myself any time to think about it, I hurled my line out for the fourth time and fished and fished and fished and fished and fished and fished and fished as hard as I could, when fancying that I felt a nibble, I hauled it in as quickly as possible and found an old sardine-tin which had become entangled in the line.

'Hastily opening the tin, all I found therein was the head of an old sprat. "Alas!" said I to myself, "is this, after all my troubles, the only food I can take to my suffering father and hungering mother and brothers and sisters; better it would have been had we never been born!" and the tears streamed down my face.

'As I bent low over my miserable catch a great shadow passed across the boat and suddenly looking up, I beheld a beautiful albatross sailing in the sky above me. No sooner did the graceful creature catch sight of the head of the sprat than it swooped down upon the tin that contained it, snatching it from my hands, and flew off with it as speedily as possible. Now it happened I had not let go my hold on the line, the other end of which was still fastened to the tin, so that in a very few minutes I felt myself lifted bodily up and whirled through the air and out to sea at a great speed. Dangling many feet beneath the great bird, on and on I was carried over the tops of the waves, in the greatest anxiety lest the marauding fowl should take a lower flight, in which case I should inevitably have been plunged into the sea and drowned.

'How many miles we travelled thus it would be impossible for me to tell, but at length my arms grew tired of holding on and supporting my weight, and I began to fear every moment that I should slip off into the sea, when I beheld a fishing-boat in the distance, right in our course. Hoping that we should reach it before my strength gave out I anxiously watched the vessel as we gradually drew near. At last I found myself directly over the boat, and shutting my eyes, I let go my hold on the line, and dropped down right

THE CAMP-FOLLOWERS

I FISHED AND FISHED AND FISHED

on to a pile of fish in the middle of the deck, sending them flying in all directions amongst the astonished fisherman.

'My remarkable appearance amongst them had the most astonishing effect upon the fishermen. They one and all leapt into the sea, and notwithstanding my endeavours to entice them back to the boat, and to explain to them my sudden descent upon their vessel, the affrighted creatures swam off to the distant shore, which, let us hope, they reached in safety.

'Looking around me I now discovered, to my great joy, that the boat was full of the finest fish, so, seizing the oars, I turned her head towards home, where I arrived with my prize on the following morning, after a hard night's work, rowing the heavily-laden craft to shore.

'The rejoicings were great, as you may well imagine, when my good parents and brothers and sisters beheld me again, for all had given me up for lost, our old boat having been washed ashore the previous evening. A great meal of fish was prepared as soon as possible, at which we all ate heartily after so long a fast, and the old gentleman's condition was greatly improved by the meal.

'Long before the large supply of food had been consumed, the good living and comfort had restored our dad's health, and he was able to resume his fishing. Being now so much better equipped with the fine boat in which I had returned, and with the splendid tackle we discovered therein, good luck always attended his fishing and we never wanted any more.

'In the course of time it became necessary that their children should all leave them and seek their fortunes, and only yesterday morning, with many tears, we bade adieu to our kind-hearted parents and started on our journey.'

The young strangers were now all thoroughly

THE CAMP-FOLLOWERS

refreshed by their breakfast, and learning the nature of the campaign upon which the King and his army were engaged, willingly offered their assistance as camp-followers, or in any other way that they might be useful. The King very gratefully accepted their services, and before resuming the march the whole army went out of their way and visited the kindly fisherman. The King was pleased to confer many honours on the old fellow, and, before leaving him, promised to look after his numerous family, and in the future to provide for all their wants.

THE SIEGE OF TROY

THE SIEGE OF TROY

EARLY one fine morning, before the soldiers had arisen, the King, in a very excited state, called his general to his bedside and, pointing through the opening of his tent, said:—

'Bill, can you see, far away upon the horizon, that little point of light?' And Bill, straining his eyes in the direction indicated, was indeed able to detect a little flash, as though the sun were shining upon a cucumber frame many miles away.

'Well,' said the old man, 'that is the reflection of the sun upon the dome of my palace in Troy.'

THE SIEGE OF TROY

Bill, delighted that at last they were nearing their journey's end, went off and awakened the camp with the glad news, and all came running out and gazed in the direction of Troy; and so heartened were the brave fellows at the sight that they gave three resounding cheers.

Their eagerness to be off was so great that there was no breakfast that morning, and soon performing a hurried toilet, and speedily packing up their sticks, they were on the move once more. The King's excitement knew no bounds and, after distributing amongst his followers the contents of his pocket, he insisted on climbing out of his chariot, and giving each of his officers in turn a ride therein. Having travelled some little way, the King suddenly called a halt, and held up his hand for silence, and then, in the clear air, could be heard the bells of Troy! More excited than ever, the King now took off his crown, and removing some of the jewels with the pen-knife which Bill had presented to him on his birthday, gave one to each of his chief officers.

In a little time the towers of Troy came into view, on the further edge of the great plain they were crossing, and the elated King, quite beside himself with joy and expectation at this glorious sight, stood upon the seat of his chariot and danced, much to the alarm of Boadicea, who was wheeling him. He then sat down again, and, taking off his slippers, he threw them, one by one, as high into the air as he could, and caught

THE SIEGE OF TROY

them as they descended. As they came nearer and nearer to their goal the old fellow's spirits rose to such a pitch that something really had to be done, so the musician was told-off to play soothing tunes to him, and in time the excitable creature calmed down, only, however, to break out again when they halted that night before the walls of Troy. At last, to keep him quiet once and for all, and out of everybody's way, they put him to bed with a soothing-draught made up by the doctor.

The approach of the gallant fellows had been closely observed from the watch-towers of the city, and, in consequence, they found the gates fast closed when they halted before them. And, as nothing could be done that night, they fixed up their camp and retired to rest.

On the following morning, Bill sent the merchant's wife as an ambassadress into the city, to demand its instant surrender, and very gladly she undertook the task.

'This is quite in my line,' said she, as she knocked for admittance at the gate, through which she was admitted after a little delay. Bill waited anxiously for her reappearance, hoping that the King of Persia would be wise enough to give up the city without further trouble, but suddenly a great roar resounded from the other side of the walls, and almost immediately afterwards the ambassadress, with tufts of the Persian King's hair held between her clenched fingers, was thrown out of the gates.

Closely observed from the watch towers

THE SIEGE OF TROY

'There's nothing for it now,' thought Bill, 'but to lay siege to the place,' and he at once proceeded to walk round the city and examine the nature of the ground; after which he mustered his whole force before him, and disposed them according to the accompanying plan:—

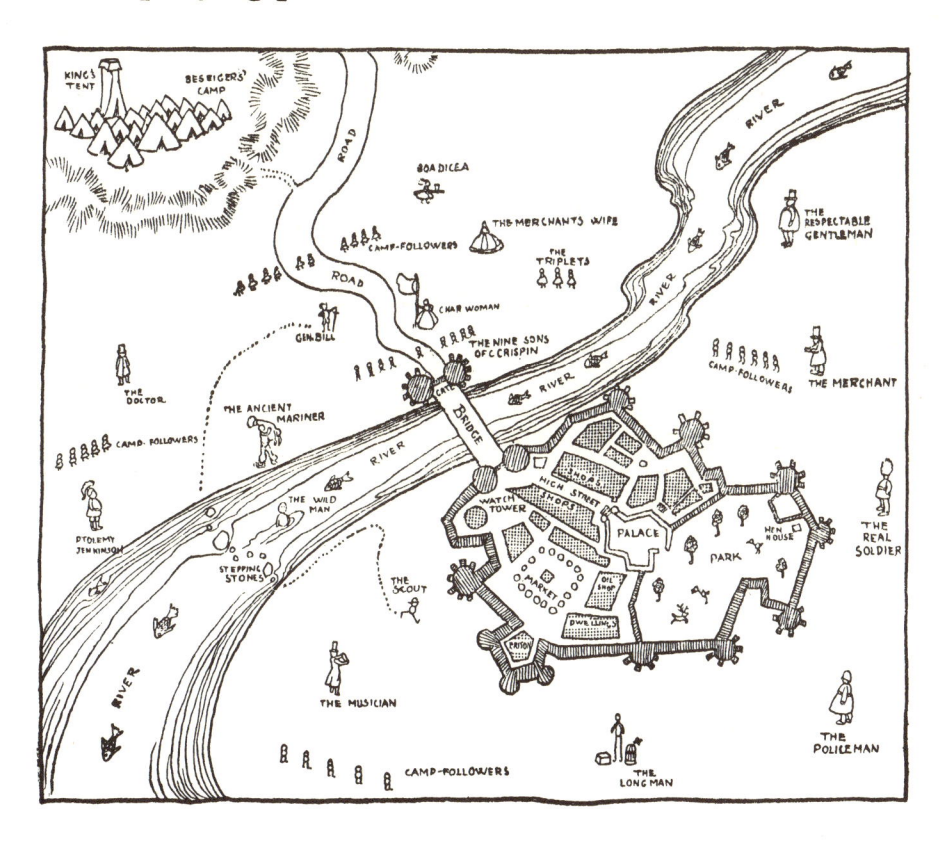

In this way Bill completely surrounded the city, allowing no provisions of any kind to enter, and prepared to wait until the inhabitants had exhausted all their stores, and could hold out no longer.

THE SIEGE OF TROY

These were the instructions of General Bill to his army, to be faithfully carried out during the siege:—

1. That the King was not to be allowed out of his tent on any account, in spite of his impatience.
2. That, with the exception of the general and the scout, no warrior was allowed, without his officer's permission, to leave his post, day or night, during the siege, and if any one were discovered sleeping without one eye open, his allowance of sugar for porridge next morning was to be stopped.
3. That the scout was to be continually on the move.
4. That Boadicea was to prepare all the meals, and that at each meal time she was to take the food she had cooked to the soldiers (an extra large portion being always reserved for the King).
5. That every morning, with breakfast, she was to take to each his boots brightly polished, a bowl of hot water to wash in, and a comb, and that every evening she should bring them their slippers and their night-shirts.

For three years the siege went on, in quite a peaceful and, at times, even a pleasant way, with no sign at all of the Trojans feeling any discomfort; in fact, since the Merchant's Wife had been turned from

THE SIEGE OF TROY

the city, not a sound had been heard from within the walls.

Now it happened one morning, about this time, that the gates, to every one's surprise, were thrown open, and a messenger, with a flag of truce, came forth. The poor fellow looked hungry enough, indeed, yet the Merchant's Wife roughly seized upon the famished creature, much to his annoyance, and brought him to the general. Bill, hoping that he had come with an offer from the King of Persia to surrender the city, joyfully handed the young man a chair and a biscuit, and, before allowing him to speak, insisted on his eating a bowl of hot porridge. When he had hungrily demolished the food, Bill kindly invited him to deliver his message, which, in a hesitating manner, he thus proceeded to do:—

'The King of Persia sends greetings to his dear old friend, the King of Troy, and wishes to assure him that he bears no ill-will towards him. On the contrary, his happiest moments are spent in recalling those far-off times when, as young children, they played the livelong day together, in good-will and friendliness. He also begs him, for a few minutes, to allow his natural kindness to overcome his enmity, and send his old friend, now faint with hunger, enough suet to make just a little pudding for himself.

Bill, a trifle disappointed, took the message to the King of Troy, who seemed very much affected on hearing it.

THE SIEGE OF TROY

THESE PARCELS WERE NOW LABELLED

'Give the old fellow a cracknel,' roared he, 'and tell him that if he surrenders the city at once, he can have as nice a snack of dinner as he could wish.'

The messenger returned to the city with the message and the cracknel, and Bill waited all through the day and night, but no word came from the city.

After breakfast next morning, when, as Bill thought, the King of Persia would be feeling hungry, he called to him the nine stout sons of Crispin and Chloe and then summoned to him the Merchant's Wife and the Sicilian Char-woman, and between them they managed to wrap up each of the brave lads in brown paper, properly secured with strong string, making nine very neat parcels. The general had previously instructed the brave fellows how to act at the right moment, and in the meantime to remain perfectly still. These parcels were now labelled severally lemon cheese cake, fairy cakes, rock cakes, Jumbles, raspberry noyeau,

THE SIEGE OF TROY

mince pies, Pontefract cakes and peppermint cushions, and then all neatly piled upon the King's wheeling-chair, which Bill had borrowed for the purpose.

Solemnly preceded by Bill, the Merchant's Wife and the Char-woman (being the two strongest people in the forces) now wheeled the chair up to the gates, in front of which they emptied its contents.

The hungry Trojans had observed their approach, from the walls above which could now be seen innumerable heads popping up and down, and no sooner did they see what the chair was supposed to contain than they climbed down, and without any hesitation opened the gates. Bill then spoke to the Trojans in the following words :—

'The King of Troy sends greetings to the King of Persia and hearing that his stores are exhausted, and, although at war with him, not wishing that he should suffer any serious discomfort, begs his acceptance of these provisions.' Bill and the two ladies now retired with the empty wheeling-chair and took up their position before the walls once more.

In the meanwhile the parcels were taken into the city and presented to the King of Persia who was then sitting, with the whole of his court, hungrily wondering what was going to happen next. The parcels were heaped up before him, and he could hardly conceal his delight and eagerness to begin on the victuals at once. All his courtiers too seemed quite inclined to forget their manners and help them-

THE SIEGE OF TROY

selves before they were asked. The King now took up the largest parcel, labelled Pontefract cakes, which happened to contain Hannibal, when at a given signal each one of the courageous young fellows broke from his confinement and at once set on those around him. Hannibal and Noah seized the Persian King and bound him securely with some of the string from the parcels; each of the other brave sons of Crispin bound some minister or courtier in the same way, and the rest of the court fled from the palace in abject terror.

The nine lads now gave chase, and the panic which possessed the affrighted courtiers spread, in no time, through the city, and the whole of the inhabitants were soon fleeing before the infuriated fellows.

Possessed with the idea that their pursuers were in much greater force than they really were, the scared wretches made for the gates of the city, out of which they ran as hard as they could. Bill, the General, wisely allowed them to pass through his lines, which they did in the maddest terror, and then fled far away over the plain, as the besieging forces once more closed in around the city.

Seeing that the gates still remained open, Bill now marshalled his gallant army, and in one grand procession led them into the city.

In front of all solemnly marched the General; then the Real Soldier; then the Merchant's Wife; then the Sicilian Char-woman, proudly waving her flag; then followed a number of Bill's charges, the Ancient

AND PACKED HIM OFF TO PERSIA

Mariner, the Doctor, Camp-followers, the Musician playing triumphant music on his concertina, more Camp-followers, the Respectable Gentleman, the Scout, the Wild Man, yet more Camp-followers, the Merchant, and, last of all, preceded by the graceful Triplets, came the proud and glad old King himself, wheeled in great state by the faithful Boadicea, and guarded by the principal policeman of Troutpeg. The nine stout sons of Crispin, together with the remaining children, formed a guard of honour, extending from the city gates as far as the front door of the Palace, into which the excited and Royal old creature entered at last amid the cheers of his gallant followers.

His first act was to release the King of Persia, and after accepting very graciously his humble and sincere apologies for his unkindness, the clement old fellow gave him a good breakfast and packed him off to Persia. In a like kindly manner he treated the courtiers, after they had all suitably begged his pardon; and the inhabitants, who came trooping back as soon as they heard how graciously the rightful King was behaving, one and all clamoured to shake the delighted old monarch by the hand and pay their homage to him.

Thus, after all his trials and privations, this Royal and kindly creature was restored to his throne. The crown was done up and beautifully polished, and the old King once more crowned in great state. To show his gratitude to his brave and faithful followers he

THE SIEGE OF TROY

TROY BECAME THE HAPPIEST TOWN

appointed them all (with the exception of the Triplets, who soon returned to Blowdripping) to places of honour in his court. Thus :—

BILL, ...	Commander-in-chief of the Army.
THE REAL SOLDIER, . .	General under Bill.
THE SCOUT, . . .	Officer of the Army.
NINE SONS OF CRISPIN, .	Bodyguard to the King.
THE CAMP-FOLLOWERS AND OTHERS, ...	The Army.
BOADICEA, ...	Royal Housekeeper.
ANCIENT MARINER, . .	Admiral of the Fleet.

THE SIEGE OF TROY

Sicilian Char-woman,	Head Char-woman to Royal Household.
The Merchant's Wife,	Superintendent of the Prison.
The Doctor,	Court Physician.
Ptolemy Jenkinson,	King's Valet.
Respectable Gentleman,	Master of Good Behaviour to the Royal Household.
Long Man,	Hall Porter at Royal Palace.
Musician,	Court Musician.
Wild Man,	Park Keeper.
Policeman,	Preserver of the Peace.

With such a gallant court and brave army around him the dear old man was saved from further troubles in his State during the remainder of his long and happy reign. In fact Troy became the very happiest town in the world, and the old King's noble followers were so contented with their lot that they never again left the city of Troy.

THE END